5TH EDITION

EFFECTIVE LAW ENFORCEMENT REPORT WRITING

LARRY E. HOLTZ

LexisNexis®
Gould Publications™

QUESTIONS ABOUT THIS PUBLICATION?

For CUSTOMER SERVICE ASSISTANCE concerning replacement pages,
shipments, billing, reprint permission, or other matters,

please call Customer Service Department at 800-833-9844
email *customer.support@lexisnexis.com*
or visit our interactive customer service website at *www.lexisnexis.com/printcdsc*

For EDITORIAL **content questions** concerning this publication,

please call 800-446-3410 ext. 7447
or email: *LLP.CLP@lexisnexis.com*

For **information on other LEXISNEXIS MATTHEW BENDER publications**,

please call us at 800-223-1940
or visit our online bookstore at *www.lexisnexis.com/bookstore*

ISBN: 1-4224-0438-2

Matthew Bender & Company, Inc.
Editorial Offices
P.O. Box 7587
Charlottesville, VA 22906-7587
800-446-3410
www.lexisnexis.com

Product Number 7506211

(Pub. 75062)

Preface

One of the most important parts of the law enforcement function is report writing. Too often, unfortunately, relatively little time and attention is devoted to the planning and preparation of a top quality, effective report. In practice, too many law enforcement officers look upon the task of report writing as distasteful–a necessary evil to be hastily performed.

The formal reports written by law enforcement officers often become part of an official record, which documents the history of a crime, incident or event. Indeed, nearly every dispatched service an officer performs, each crime and accident scene investigated, and any other criminal justice operation requiring that a record be made for future reference, calls for an accurately worded entry in a log or a detailed chronicle of information, commonly known as the "officer's report." While the length of these reports may vary from a single brief sentence to a very sophisticated document of many pages, each has one common purpose: to communicate information in an accurate, understandable and complete manner.

In the field, an officer's attitude and ability are judged by the people with whom the officer deals, and evaluated by his or her superiors. Sometimes the impressions are short-lived, sometimes not. The reports that the officer writes, however, are quite different–they are far more indelible and long-lasting.

To be effective, formal reports should always be written with the intended audience or potential reader in mind. Such reports are often used to determine future courses of action. Therefore, they must be taken seriously. An officer's overall knowledge, efficiency and effectiveness are inevitably, if not invariably, appraised on the basis of the reports prepared. Such reports may be viewed by peers, supervisors, the media, social service agencies, and insurance companies. In the criminal justice system, an officer's report will be read and analyzed by prosecutors, defense attorneys and judges. Consequently, the quality and effectiveness of an officer's report can help to convict the guilty and respect the rights of crime victims.

Without adequate report writing skills, a public safety officer cannot be effective in today's criminal justice arena. This text, *Effective Law Enforcement Report Writing*, provides an easy-to-read set of report-writing guidelines and standards for today's law enforcement officer. In Part I, the text sets forth, in ten easy steps, the ways in which any official report can be immediately improved. The goal is to provide the professional in the field with the knowledge, skills and ability to prepare well-written reports that are clearer, more coherent, more complete and more easily understood.

Part II of *Effective Law Enforcement Report Writing* contains hundreds of practice questions, problems and exercises for classroom use, designed for the student and for law enforcement trainers and criminal justice educators to use to test a student's knowledge of the subject. In addition, those preparing for any law enforcement or corrections "entry level" or "promotional" exam will find these practice questions and exercises extraordinarily valuable for exam preparation and review of this subject.

Part III of the text provides an extensive report writing "Reference Section," which sets forth commonly misused and misspelled words in law enforcement, along with a study guide containing commonly used "roots," "prefixes," and "suffixes."

The Author

Larry E. Holtz received his Bachelor of Arts Degree in Criminal Justice from Temple University, Philadelphia, Pennsylvania, graduating Summa Cum Laude. In December of 1988, he received his Juris Doctorate from Temple University School of Law, graduating in the top ten percent of his class.

Formerly a Sergeant of Detectives with the Atlantic City Police Department, a Deputy Attorney General and an assistant county prosecutor, Mt. Holtz is presently an attorney specializing in police administrative matters, the Municipal Prosecutor for several towns in the southern New Jersey area, and the Executive Director of *Holtz Learning Centers, Ltd*. He is also a certified police instructor, providing training at numerous police training academies in New Jersey and Pennsylvania, and is an Adjunct Professor of Law at Widener University School of Law, Wilmington, Delaware, and an Adjunct Professor of Criminal Justice at Rowan University, Glassboror, New Jersey.

Mr. Holtz is the author of the *Contemporary Criminal Procedure: Court Decisions for Law Enforcement*, the *New Jersey Law Enforcement Handbook*, the *Pennsylvania Law Enforcement Handbook*, and *Criminal Evidence for Law Enforcement Officers*. He is published in the *Pennsylvania Law Journal-Reporter*, the *Journal of Criminal Law and Criminology*, and the *Dickinson Law Review*. In addition, he is the co-author of the *Texas Law Enforcement Handbook* and the *Supervision of Police Personnel Study Guide*.

Mr. Holtz is a member of the Bar in New Jersey, Pennsylvania, and the District of Columbia.

Holtz Learning Centers

As the Executive Director of Police Training for Holtz Learning Centers, Ltd., Mr. Holtz provides a wide variety of basic and advanced training to law enforcement officials in New Jersey and Pennsylvania. His seminars cover such topics as (1) The Laws of Arrest, Search and Seizure (basic and advanced); (2) Criminal and Motor Vehicle Law Updates; (3) Interviews, Confessions and *Miranda*; (4) Kinetic Reading (designed to supercharge one's reading speed, comprehension and memory); (5) Investigative and Operational Report Writing; and (6) Principles of Police Supervision and Management. In addition, Mr. Holtz conducts comprehensive executive development courses designed to prepare law enforcement officials for the move up to sergeant, lieutenant, captain, inspector, deputy chief and chief.

For more information regarding specialized training, write to Holtz Learning Centers, Ltd., P.O. Box 543, Woodbine, New Jersey 08270, or contact the main office at 1-800-320-8653, or at **holtzlc@verizon.net**, or visit our website at **holtzlearningcenters.com**.

Table of Contents

Table of Contents *(cont.)*

EFFECTIVE LAW ENFORCEMENT REPORT WRITING

by
Larry E. Holtz

INTRODUCTION

The hallmark of the competent law enforcement officer is the ability to record his or her observations and actions in a clear, concise and readily understandable manner. One of the means through which an officer's observations and actions are recorded is the "Incident" or "Operations Report." Another is the "Investigation" or "Supplementary Investigation Report." These are the official documents which provide the spark which fires the other components of the criminal justice system into action. Properly executed, the criminal justice process is initiated with Due Process and Fundamental Fairness; without them, no formal process begins. Consequently, the officer's report is an extremely powerful tool. It is powerful because it makes things happen—it invokes the entire criminal justice process, and accordingly, should not be approached in a lax or haphazard manner.

In the pages that follow, a set of guidelines is set forth to aid the law enforcement officer's official reporting. The "guidelines" are set forth in the form of ten general commandments. When The Ten Commandments of Effective Law Enforcement Reporting are carefully followed, you will not only find the quality of your official reports improving but, in time, you will be turning out highly improved, professionally clear, concise and perfectly understandable reports.

Always bear in mind, the content and appearance of your official report reflects both upon your employer as a professional law enforcement agency, and upon you—as an individual and as a representative of that agency. It can strongly suggest the presence of credibility; or it can strongly suggest the absence of credibility. The reflections and suggestions are up to you. In the long run, you will always be judged by how effectively you get across what happened—in the "written word." Consequently, when you sign your name on the bottom of your report, you tell every other person in the criminal justice system the type of person you are and the type of organization you represent.

With this in mind, we have . . .

PART I

THE TEN COMMANDMENTS OF EFFECTIVE LAW ENFORCEMENT REPORTING

Never Fail to Properly Document Your Actions and Observations

From the minor transportation notation in your vehicle patrol log to the most involved criminal incident report, your actions and observations must be recorded. Naturally, the more significant the action taken, the more involved the report. Even if you believe the action does not constitute "official action," *if it affects the life, liberty or property of another person in any significant way, document your actions and observations.* It is all too easy, at a later date, to connect any of your actions—official or other—to your authoritative position as a law enforcement officer. Documentation is the keynote; it is your best protection, so make it work *for* you, not against you.

There are many situations in which an officer may become involved where it does not immediately appear that a written report is necessary. For example, the situation in which an officer is not dispatched to a particular scene but merely responds on his or her own initiative to assist in "checking the area." Here, many officers would believe that a written report is unnecessary if the area "checks negative." This is a serious misconception. At trial this "negative evidence" can prove to be just as vital to the government's case as any other evidence presented.

Whenever an officer engages in a crime-scene search, an area search for evidence of crime, or an area search for the purpose of locating possible suspects or named wanted individuals, the officer is gathering evidence. If the search is productive, whatever the officer finds—the "positive" evidence—certainly must be documented in an official report. If the search is not productive, however, whatever the officer does *not* find—the "negative" evidence, should also be documented in a similar fashion. Significantly, there are many times at trial when these *negative reports* may serve to counter defenses raised by a defendant. One such example is the defense of "self-defense," where the defendant alleges in an aggravated assault prosecution that the victim provoked the attack with a weapon, but discarded the weapon *before* the police arrived. If the prosecution can present official documentation and testimony from those officers who responded to, and searched, the area of the crime, and such documentation and testimony demonstrates not only that the immediate area of the crime scene was thoroughly searched but also an area beyond the crime scene covering a distance beyond which the victim could have possibly thrown a weapon, the defendant will then naturally have a very difficult time establishing his defense.

Eyewitness identification is another area where negative reports serve to enhance the investigation and strengthen the credibility of the procedure. In this respect, the act of showing a suspect to a victim or witness shortly after the crime for the purpose of identification should always be documented in an official report—whether identification is or is not made. The same procedure applies when an officer displays either a photo array or an in-person lineup to a victim or witness. Whenever an Incident or Operations Report documents that a positive eyewitness identification has been preceded by one or more showings in which the witness made no identification (because the perpetrator was not in the lineup), the government's case respecting the reliability of the ultimate identification of the defendant may be enhanced.

An investigative detention and protective search—the *Terry*[1] stop and frisk—is a legitimate and widely used police procedure. It is also a procedure that directly impacts on the liberty of an individual. The detention is conducted for the purpose of investigating an officer's reasonable and articulable suspicion that the person to be detained is, or has been, engaged in criminal activity. The frisk is performed to assure the officer that the person with whom he or she is dealing is not armed with a weapon.[2] If, during the course of the investigative detention, the officer confirms his or her suspicion of criminal activity—that is, develops enough additional facts to establish probable cause, an arrest may be made. There are, however, many times when the investigative detention discloses no criminal activity, and the frisk produces no weapon. The person must then be permitted to go on his or her way.[3] Is a report necessary?

If you value your career, it is. The failure to document an "unproductive" stop and frisk is a dangerous and unprofessional practice. Although

---

1. *Terry v. Ohio*, 391 U.S. 1, 88 S.Ct. 1868 (1968).

2. *See Terry* at 8, 88 S.Ct. at 1873 (The frisk is "essential to the officer's investigative duties, for without it, the answer to the police officer's inquiries] may be a bullet[.]").

3. *See e.g., Berkemer v. McCarty*, 468 U.S. 420, 439-40, 104 S.Ct. 3138, 3151 (1984) ("[U]nless the detainee's answers provide the officer with probable cause to arrest him, he must be released.").

the interference with the person's liberty seems minimal, the stop and frisk is nonetheless a law-enforcement practice considered by the courts to be a "far from inconsiderable intrusion upon the sanctity of the person."[4] It is also an activity that can result in your being named as a defendant in a lawsuit. Six months or a year (or more) down the road, it will be extremely difficult, if not impossible, to recreate the specific and articulable facts that constitutionally justified the stop and frisk on the day in question. The person you detained, however, probably has the events of that day burned into memory, and perhaps even documented at his or her lawyer's office. If you are called upon to account for your actions at some point in the future, a simple incident report, prepared the day of the challenged stop and frisk, will refresh your memory of the facts and circumstances that originally authorized the procedure. Such a report may also serve as the basis for your defense to such charges as false arrest, false imprisonment, or assault and battery. Indeed, the mere existence of such an incident report may serve to discourage the filing of a lawsuit, or criminal charges, against you.

As the examples illustrate, a report relating "negative evidence" carries just as much weight as any report which relates "positive evidence." Such a report may also serve as your first line of defense to any civil or criminal charges.

Additionally, the proper and complete documentation of all persons interviewed, areas checked or other similar actions can save valuable time later in the investigation. Such documentation (1) eliminates the unnecessary duplication of effort, and (2) facilitates the investigator's ability to quickly locate (and conduct supplemental interviews with) important witnesses. In this regard, it is strongly recommended that in addition to recording the names and addresses of witnesses, the officer also include (1) the home telephone number of the witness, (2) the witness' place of employment (if any) and telephone number there, and (3) the name, address and telephone number of a relative, friend or neighbor of the witness if the witness has no telephone or place of employment.

Thus, whether you are reporting the facts and circumstances surrounding a homicide, or merely documenting the presence of a hazardous traffic condition, always remember that your report is a fundamental element of police teamwork. Unless the information you have is shared with the other members of the relevant criminal justice community in a "timely" and "orderly" fashion, it is useless. Don't put it off until tomorrow. Delays of one, two or more days serve only to detract from the credibility of your report and the usefulness of your information.

---

4. *Terry* at 26, 88 *S.Ct.* at 1882.

Notes

Always Maintain Perspective

Effective official reporting must always: a. have a particular purpose, and b. respect the intelligence of its recipient or recipients. If your report serves no particular purpose, why report at all? Thus, always keep in mind the reason why you are writing, and the person or group of people who will be reading what you have written.

More often than not, the purpose of the report will be readily apparent; nonetheless, many officers tend to lose this perspective. The result is an incoherent report which leaves the reader wondering: What is he trying to tell me?

You will find it helpful, when sitting down to write your report (or for that matter, sitting down to write anything), to begin with a kind of image—a picture to carry in your mind's eye—of that person or group of people who will be reading what you have taken the time to reduce to black and white. But in order to make this picture come alive, you must ask yourself three questions. If you take the time to mentally answer these questions, you will find no difficulty whatsoever keeping a handle on the underlying purpose of the report, while at the same time respecting your particular audience by keeping the writing style framed in a form appropriate for their receipt and review.

Accordingly, "to maintain perspective", ask:

1. Why am I writing this report? [What is its purpose?]
2. Who is my audience? [To whom am I submitting this report?]
3. In what way will this report become a part of a future proceeding?

By asking and answering the third question, you will be developing a conceptual skill which permits you to see how your observations, actions and decisions—reflected in your writing—fit into the overall scheme of things, that is, the "big picture." Interestingly, analysis by reference to the "big picture" was formally utilized by the United States Supreme Court, and adopted as a doctrine of constitutional law with regard to searches and seizures in the case of *Illinois v. Gates*.[1] The Supreme Court called it: *The Totality of the Circumstances*.

---

1. 462 *U.S.* 213, 103 *S.Ct.* 2317 (1983).

Always <u>Think</u> Before You Write

This Commandment fits right in the palm of "Maintaining Perspective." Confused, vague, or ambiguous reporting results from a failure to think through the facts and circumstances which will ultimately make up the body or narrative of the report.

Many officers suffer from the disease of "diarrhea of the pen"; they let their pen do their thinking. Don't write haphazardly just to "get it done," or just to "get the detective or supervisor off your back." The practice of shortchanging your report because you are "in a hurry," or because you have "someplace better to be," can only come back to haunt you. Take your time and think!

No matter how effective you are on the street—no matter how many felony or indictable arrests you have made; no matter how many unlawfully possessed guns you have confiscated—the desired result will be lost if you cannot or will not take the time to document your actions in a way that is clear and understandable. Moreover, should your actions become the subject of a future lawsuit, your report will likely be the basis for both the plaintiff's allegations and your defense. In fact, your report may be the only formal written record of what you did and what the plaintiff did on the day in question.

Think through each portion of your report from beginning to end; then write. This will not only provide the clarity and coherence so necessary for effective official reporting, but it may also protect you should your conduct be called into question at some point in the future. Further, it may, as the below example illustrates, eliminate the need for future translation. For further help in this regard, refer to the **FIFTH COMMANDMENT.**

11

Accordingly, if you combine this **THIRD COMMANDMENT** with the **SECOND COMMANDMENT**, you will NEVER AGAIN write a report which begins in the following way:

> "On the above date and above time, we, the undersigned, gave a 53 to 52 a 49 to 56 due to some 23 with her 27 boyfriend which ended in a 26."[1]

There is a significant difference between the way in which average law enforcement officers write and the way professionals write:

Average officer: Write the report, hand it in.

Above-average officer: Write the report, edit it, rewrite it, hand it in

Exceptional officer: Write the report, edit it, rewrite it, edit it, rewrite it, hand it in

Professional: Write the report, edit it, rewrite it, edit it, rewrite it, edit it, rewrite it, edit it, rewrite it; edit it, hand it in.

The professional recognizes that in so many instances, 50 percent of the time in report writing is spent initially drafting the report; the other 50 percent of the time should be dedicated to "cleanup." Paying attention to the art of "cleanup" is just as important as the time spent in initial drafting.

---

1. Incident report submitted in reference to an aggravated assault case, occurring in Atlantic City, New Jersey. The officer in this sentence (without the numbers) stated: "On the above date and above time, we the undersigned went out of service to transport a complainant to the Medical Center due to some trouble with her intoxicated boyfriend which ended in a fight."

Take Field Notes

I 'm sure you have heard the old maxim: "An officer's notebook serves as the Law Enforcement Department's official memory." Do you still carry a notebook? Pocket-sized notebooks are really not that bulky to carry. They are, however, an indispensable part of your equipment.

More important than the maxim about the "department's memory," is *your* memory. Studies have shown that the mere act of writing something down will impress it more deeply in your memory. Don't rely on your ability to remember each particular fact or event. Chances are, you will inevitably forget something important.

Field notes are simple notations, made "in the field," that serve as a shorthand or abbreviated written record of what was seen, said or done. If taken properly, field notes will greatly reduce the risk of the inaccurate reporting of names; addresses; dates of birth; social security numbers; serial numbers; times; locations of evidence, witnesses, victims, or suspects; distances; and so on. Thereafter, your field notes serve as an index to your memory of the event in question, and as the basis for your formal report.

The mere act of field notetaking can be an "art" in its own right. Naturally, the mind works incredibly faster than your hand's ability to capture the written word. Because of this phenomenon, you should not try to write down each and every word; forget the "full sentence" (field notes only, of course). Rather, record only key phrases or "buzz words." In addition, as you write in your field notebook, be sure to leave blank spaces between the lines. Try not to use up every part of every page. You may need to insert additional facts, should they come to light, or correct information which may have been inaccurately noted. Later, a quick review of the information entered in your field notebook will refresh your memory.

For example, even though you were not the reporting officer who created the following page of field notes, see if you can picture what happened:

3/4/02; 02:30

Night/Clear/Dry

Good Street Lighting

Victim - John Doe/wallet ID

Down/Bleeding - forehead

Weapon???

Gun? Knife? Rock?

Broken glass around

V's head

Weap. - Bottle

Suspect? Witnesses?

Assist. - Ofs. Jones

Burke, K-9 Wells

Sgt. Holmes

When sitting down to write the final report, the simple exercise of reviewing your field notes will keep you from jumping around the facts without direction; it will permit you to account for the entire episode which is the subject of your report; and it will help you to include all the pertinent details, the review of which—at a later date—will permit you to remember everything that happened with regard to that particular case. Moreover, when field notes are accurately written at the time of observation, they will add a great deal to the writer's credibility; not only as a professional in the field, but as a witness at any future legal proceeding. This is most apparent when, as a witness, you are questioned about your memory of particular facts or details of the event. Here, the act of making reference to the names, locations, key phrases or "buzz words" in your original field notes is proper, and a highly persuasive technique; it indicates documentation of your actions and observations at a time when they were fresh in your mind.

This does not mean to suggest, however, that field notes must *always* be saved for future proceedings. So long as you carefully and fully incorporate your field notes into your formal report, the field notes may be discarded. Two words of caution: First, although there is no general legal mandate calling for the preservation of most forms of field notes, your department may have a rule or regulation requiring it. Second, as a matter of standard practice and procedure, many law enforcement agencies and courts require the retention of an officer's or agent's "rough notes" which document an interview with a prospective witness,[1] or which contain information that is exculpatory in nature—information that is favorable and material to the defense.[2] Field notes which do not contain such items may, after full and complete incorporation into the formal report, be discarded.[3]

An officer's testimony concerning the destruction of his or her rough/field notes should be positive and deliberate. Consider the following:

Cross-Examination

By Mr. Defense Attorney:

> Q. Now officer, you were taught in the police academy to always take field notes, were you not?
> A. We were taught to take field notes whenever the situation reasonably permits the taking of notes.
>
> Q. Officer, you were dispatched to the alleged crime scene?
> A. Yes.

---

1. *See e.g., United States v. Vella*, 562 F.2d 275, 276 (3rd Cir. 1977), where the court noted that it is "now the policy of the Federal Bureau of Investigation to preserve rough notes of interviews," recognizing the requirement, under the Jencks Act, 18 U.S.C. §3500(e)(1), for the government to preserve written statements made by a witness which are "signed or otherwise adopted or approved by him." *See also United States v. Lonardo*, 350 F.2d 523 (6th Cir. 1965) (case reversed because federal agents destroyed their original notes in an apparent attempt to avoid the production required under the Jencks Act); *United States v. Ammar*, 714 F.2d 238, 259 & n.19 (3rd Cir. 1983) ("[T]he government must retain and, upon motion, make available to the district court, both the rough notes and the drafts of reports of its agents" containing "Jencks Act" statements.).

2. *See Brady v. Maryland*, 373 U.S. 83, 83 S.Ct. 1194 (1963); *United States v. Hill*, 976 F.2d 132, 143-45 (3rd Cir. 1992) (government must produce all exculpatory evidence which includes both "materials... that go to the heart of the defendant's guilt or innocence and materials that might affect the jury's judgment of the credibility of a crucial prosecution witness"). *See also United States v. Ramos*, 27 F.3d 65, 70 (3rd Cir. 1994) (noting that it is now the policy of the DEA to require retention of such rough notes).

3. *See Killian v. United States*, 368 U.S. 231, 82 S.Ct. 302, 308 (1961) (so long as the notes are destroyed in good faith and in accord with normal practice, "their destruction [does] not constitute an impermissible destruction of evidence"). *See also United States v. Comulada*, 340 F.2d 449, 451 (2nd Cir. 1965) (destruction of notes, which an officer thought were no longer useful in the case, did not constitute a basis for reversal). *Wright v. State*, 501 P.2d 1360, 1371 (Alaska 1972) (police department's pre-trial act of destroying police captain's notes taken during interview with a prospective government witness found to be "in good faith, without the intent to avoid production," and therefore "not a ground for reversal"); *State v. Zenquis*, 251 N.J.Super. 358, 370, 598 A.2d 245 (App.Div. 1991) (officer's destruction of his notes "did not impair the defendant's ability to defend"; approving, however, an instruction to the jury that if it found that the officer destroyed his notes at a time when he knew the case was proceeding to trial, it could infer that the notes contained information inconsistent with the witness's trial testimony), *aff'd* 131 N.J. 84, 618 A.2d 335 (1993).

Q. You arrived at the scene quickly?
A. Yes I did.

Q. You spoke with several persons there?
A. Yes.

Q. Well, that situation certainly was one which provided an opportunity for the taking of field notes, wasn't it?
A. Yes.

Q. You took field notes, didn't you officer?
A. Yes.

Q. Now officer, you were taught in the police academy to include every important fact in your notes, weren't you?
A. We were taught that the purpose of the field notes is to help refresh our recollection for the writing of the formal incident or investigation report.

Q. Your notes documented what the witnesses at the scene told you?
A. Yes.

Q. You gave those notes to the prosecutor?
A. No.

Q. No? What did you do with your notes?
A. After carefully and meticulously incorporating the information contained in the notes into my formal report, I discarded them.

Q. You threw them away?
A. Yes I did.

Q. Why did you throw them away?
A. The rough notes are made for the purpose of facilitating the writing of the formal police report. After the information contained in the rough notes is carefully transferred into the formal report, the rough notes are discarded as a matter of standard practice and procedure.

The Crime Scene Sketch

Also a part of field notetaking is the "crime scene sketch." Crime scene sketching can become imperative, particularly in those departments which do not have a separate identification unit or specialized crime scene personnel. Sketches not only assist you when you sit down to write your formal report, but they also serve as a unique documentary exhibit at trial. Generally, juries take in all the testimony at trial "aurally," that is, only by "listening"; and studies have shown that the average person can only listen "effectively" for about fifty minutes "unless otherwise stimulated." As a result, if a witness has this "other stimulation," such as a sketch or diagram to show the jury, this will not only make his testimony more believable and credible, but he or she, as a witness, will be more interesting, informative, and much more rememberable to the jury.

Many officers fall into the trap of believing that sketches are not necessary when the crime scene is being processed and photographed by crime-scene personnel. This is dead wrong. As a documentary form of evidence, the crime scene sketch provides a graphic display of the scene (in whole or in part) with accurate measurements of distances between objects. Crime scene sketches assist in (1) accurately portraying the physical facts of the incident; (2) relating the sequence of events at the scene; (3) establishing the precise location and relationship of objects and evidence at the scene; (4) helping to create a mental picture of the scene for those not present; (5) interviewing and interrogating persons connected with the crime or incident; (6) creating a permanent record of the scene; and (7) presenting the case in court.[4]

Crime scene sketches differ from crime scene photographs in several respects. First, from an evidentiary point of view, crime scene photographs fall more neatly into the category of documentary evidence. Crime scene sketches have attributes of both documentary and demonstrative evidence, particularly when reproduced or recreated in court as a *demonstration* for the jury. Next, while photographs have the capacity to reproduce the scene in detail, and are extraordinarily valuable at crime scenes, they may, at times, tend to distort angles, distances and relationships between objects and evidence at the scene. Also, photographs do not show items behind other items and do not show measurements or accurate distances between objects and evidence. On the other hand, the crime scene sketch, as a supplement, brings out what the camera cannot "see"—it provides a clear and concise description of all items of evidence at the crime scene, their relationship to each other, the distances between objects and the movement of witnesses and suspects. In addition, unnecessary detail at a crime scene can be eliminated or reduced on a sketch, allowing for each crime scene sketch to demonstrate precise areas of interest.

Rough sketches and formal or "finished" sketches. The preliminary or "rough" crime scene sketch is drawn by the investigator or crime scene technician as he or she takes field notes. It is the first diagram of the scene and is generally not drawn to scale. Naturally, during the rough-sketching process, evidence should not be disturbed or moved from its original position until photographs and accurate measurements are taken. In this respect, as a matter of evidence law, an object that has been once moved

---

4. Mauriello, *Criminal Investigation Handbook: Strategy, Law and Science* (Matthew Bender 1998), at 7-17.

cannot be returned to its *exact original* position without raising serious credibility issues.

Later, the formal, more detailed or "finished" crime scene scaled drawing is drafted from the investigator's field notes, "rough" sketches and photographs of the scene. It is recommended that both the rough and finished sketches be preserved as both may constitute evidence at a later court hearing.

Types of Sketches

The rectangular-coordinate method of sketching is an easy method for locating objects and evidence in a square or rectangular room. This method employs two adjacent walls as fixed points from which distances are measured at right angles. Objects are located by measuring from one wall at right angles and then from the adjacent wall at right angles.[5]

The baseline method is another coordinate measurement technique which establishes a baseline from one fixed point to another. This method requires that a straight line be drawn from one fixed point to another, from which measurements are taken at right angles. Measurements are then taken along the baseline to a point at right angles to the object to be portrayed.[6]

The triangulation sketch is used most often in outdoor settings where there are no readily identifiable reference points, such as edges of fields or roads, to use as baselines. Triangulation sketching employs "straight-line measures from two fixed objects to the evidence to create a triangle with the evidence in the angle formed by the two straight lines. The degree of the angle formed at the location of the object or evidence can then be measured with a protractor."[7]

The projection sketch is a two-dimensional diagram which depicts the full crime scene with all relevant objects in the area. The distance between each object is shown.

The cross-projection sketch is helpful when it is necessary to locate objects on walls or show the relationship between evidence on the floor and evidence on the walls. Where most sketches will show the crime scene in two dimensions, the cross-projection method of sketching portrays the scene in three dimensions to allow a better analysis of the evidence. The cross-projection sketch of a room is drawn as though the viewer is straight above it, looking down at it. "In effect, the room is flattened out much like a box cut down at the four corners and opened out flat."[8] The floor and walls are then presented as though they were one flat surface.

---

5. Bennett and Hess, *Criminal Investigation* (West/Wadsworth 1998), at 60.
6. *Id.*
7. *Id.* at 62.
8. *Id.*

The schematic sketch is useful to illustrate a significant chain of events, for example, the path of a bullet, or movement of suspects, victims or vehicles.[9]

The elevation sketch is used when a vertical illustration of the crime scene is necessary. Such a sketch is helpful when an outside area with hills and valleys, or a two-story building must be shown.[10]

Field Notes Facilitate Suspect/Witness Interviews

Field notetaking can also serve as an important aid to interviewers. For example if an arrest is made in the field and the suspect is brought to the department's Detective Bureau or Investigations Office, many times the detective or investigator will conduct the formal questioning *before* the Incident or Operations Report is written. Your field notes, at this time, can be an extremely valuable asset to the person conducting the interview; it serves as a "detail reminder," and makes the interview significantly more productive.

The notes may also serve to safeguard a particular defendant's constitutional rights, and at the same time, save a confession. For example, if an officer, after effecting an arrest in the field, reads the arrestee his *Miranda* rights and the arrestee immediately invokes either his right to remain silent or his right to counsel, those facts must be documented and relayed to the detective or investigator *before* any subsequent questioning of the arrestee. It is all too often that during the haste and hustle of a dangerous arrest, the arrestee's statement that he "doesn't want to talk," or that "a lawyer might be a good idea," does not get documented in the arresting officer's field notes, and never gets relayed to the investigator or detective. Should the accused be thereafter questioned, any statements or confessions received may well be suppressed[11]—particularly if the arrestee asked for a lawyer.[12]

---

9. *Mauriello* at 7-22.

10. *Id.* at 7-23.

11. See *Michigan v. Mosley*, 324 *U.S.* 96, 96 *S.Ct.* 321 (1975), where the United States Supreme Court held that once a person in custody has indicated a desire to remain silent, law enforcement officers must "scrupulously honor" the desire by cutting off any further questioning. After a significant break in time, officers may then return to the accused to see if he has changed his mind and is willing to talk. If so, a fresh set of *Miranda* warnings should be administered and no questioning should take place until the accused voluntarily, knowingly, and intelligently waives his rights. Officers are cautioned, however, that in *Mosley*, the decision of the suspect to remain silent was held to be "scrupulously honored" based on the facts of that case where, after Mosley invoked his right to silence, (1) the police did not approach him for two hours, (2) they administered fresh *Miranda* warnings prior to resuming questioning, (3) he was questioned by different officers, and (4) he was questioned about an offense different from the one for which he was in custody.

12. See *Edwards v. Arizona*, 451 *U.S.* 477, 101 *S.Ct.* 1880 (1981), holding that once an accused in custody indicates that he would like a lawyer, there may be no questioning until he is furnished a lawyer, "unless the accused himself initiates further communication, exchanges or conversations with the [officer]." *See also Oregon v. Bradshaw*, 462 *U.S.* 1039, 102 *S.Ct.* 2830 (1983).

Field notetaking almost invariably incorporates the field interview. Field interviews should be conducted one at a time, separating the witnesses from each other as soon as possible. Be particular about the questions asked, and at no time ask leading questions. Leading questions suggest the desired answer and can cause the witness to give incorrect information. Additionally, in court, the defense attorney could object on the ground that you put your own words into the mouth of the witness. Thus, as a general rule, let the witness give his or her "own" account, that is, his or her own answers without your help, no matter how inviting or easy it is to suggest the answer you want to hear.

In most cases, it is a good practice, at the conclusion of the interview, to read your notes back to the individual. This provides the individual with an opportunity to correct mistakes or remember additional information. It also gives you an opportunity to review you notes for accuracy and ask any additional questions that may come to mind.

Finally, *what should you include in your field notebook?* Refer to the *OPERATIONS REPORT CHECKLIST* immediately following **THE FIFTH COMMANDMENT**.

Briefly Outline Before You Begin Writing Your Formal Report

The use of an outline not only makes the final report more coherent, but in addition, it serves as a *completeness tool*. It is necessary in any type of writing, and especially in official reporting, to strive for "coherence." "Coherence" is the quality of logic and order. If the report lacks a logical sequence; if the events are recorded out of their logical order, the reader will have the difficult, if not impossible, chore of figuring out what actually took place; forever begging the questions: What happened first? What happened second? Who was the first person on the scene? Who was the first officer on the scene? What's on second? The questions could go on and on.

The practice of outlining before writing a formal report invariably strengthens your report-writing skills. It is an easy and simple, yet structured, way to organize the information in your possession as you prepare to write the formal report. The outline itself serves as an *abstract* of the critical facts that must be documented. In this respect, it serves to summarize and highlight the key factual information that must be included in your formal report.

For example, when outlining the circumstances surrounding the necessary use of force to effect the arrest of a violent suspect, the following outline may be helpful:

I. HOW
   A. How the arrest was effected
      1. Suspect's actions prior to arrest
         a. Loud and verbally abusive
            (1)   (Explain how.)
            (2)   (Explain what suspect said.)
         b. Threatening and combative behavior
            (1)   (Explain exactly how suspect threatened:)
               i. Clenched fists
               ii. Assumed fighting stance
            (2)   (Explain exactly how suspect attacked officer and include the degree of the attack's intensity:)
               i. Punched officer in face
               ii. Kicked officer in groin
            (3)   (Describe any and all injuries sustained by officer.)
      2. Officer's reaction to suspect's attack
         a. (Explain the extent of force applied which was necessary to prevent further injury to the officer (or others).)
         b. (Explain the extent of force applied which was necessary to overcome the suspect's use of force.)
         c. (Include anything else of particular importance to this particular set of circumstances (*e.g.*, suspect appeared to be a martial arts specialist, etc.).)

This added detail serves to "slow the camera down" so as to permit the reader to "catch" every aspect of the suspect's violent and unlawful behavior. It will also provide complete and comprehensive evidentiary documentation necessary to support the propriety of your actions and the credibility of your explanations, should you ever have to testify about the matter in a future proceeding.

Outlining your observations and actions in a comprehensive manner will not only guarantee the completeness of your final, formal report, but it will help you to avoid rambling on about unimportant matters by forcing you to stick to, and focus upon the facts.

Assuming, then, that an outline is a necessary ingredient to the proper completion of your final report, *exactly how should you outline, and what should the outline contain?* The answer to this question may be found in the pages immediately following this Commandment. These pages contain the *OPERATIONS REPORT OUTLINE-CHECKLIST* which may be used as your model.

Department of _____

Operations Report Outline-Checklist

_____

Incident, Offense, or Crime

_____

Case Number

Purpose: _____.
Audience: _____.

____ I. WHAT
  A. Type of incident
  B. If of a criminal nature:
    1. Statutory violation (*e.g.,* burglary and theft)
    2. Code section number
    3. Prohibited conduct (elements of the offense)
      a. Acts
      b. Culpability (Intent) (noting any volunteered information)
      c. Any extenuating circumstances
  C. If other than criminal
    1. Surrounding circumstances of event
    2. Persons (or property) involved; comments; statements; etc.

____ II. WHEN
  A. Time and date of incident
  B. Time and date discovered
  C. Time and date reported
  D. Time and date victim(s) is (are) located (or identified)
  E. Time and date suspect(s) is (are) located and/or identified

23

F.   Time and date of any search
  1. Documentation of the constitutional justification
  2. Time and date a consent to search is obtained
G.   Time and date evidence is seized, marked, stored, removed, or delivered
H.   Time and date property is identified, recovered or returned
I.   Time and date of arrest(s)
J.   Time and date of *Miranda* warning administration
  1. How the arrestee(s) responded
  2. Time and date of any request for counsel
  3. Time and date of any request to remain silent

_____ III.   WHO
A.   Who is reporting?
B.   Who called the police?
C.   Who is (are) the victim(s)? Complainant(s)? Witness(es)?
D.   Who discovered the event (if different from complainant)?
E.   Who was the first person on the scene?
F.   Who was the first officer on the scene? Other officers present?
G.   Who is (are) the suspect(s)?
H.   Who has been arrested?
I.   Who is (are) the arresting officer(s)?
J.   If a search is involved, who conducted it?
K.   Who transported the suspect(s) to headquarters?
L.   Who discovered the evidence?
M.   Who seized the evidence?
N.   Who took possession of the evidence?
O.   Who transported the evidence to police headquarters?
P.   To whom was the evidence given? (chain of custody)

_____ IV.   WHERE
A.   Where did the incident occur?
B.   Where was (were) the victim(s) found?
C.   Where was (were) the suspect(s) found?
D.   Where was (were) the witness(es) situated in relation to the event?

  E. Where did any identifications take place?
    Noting particularly:
    1. Type of area;
    2. Lighting;
    3. Length of confrontation;
    4. The identifying party's degree of attention;
    5. Whether confrontation was a face-to-face, side view, etc.;
    6. Whether the person making the identification was the victim or a bystander;
    7. Whether the suspect's appearance matches any previously-given descriptions;
    8. The identifying party's degree of certainty;
    9. The length of time between the crime and the identification; and
    10. Any other unique features of the identification.
  F. Where did the arrest(s) take place?
  G. Where did any searches or seizures take place?
  H. Where was the property, evidence or contraband found?

_____   V. WHY
  A. Motive
  B. Opportunity and Ability
  C. Desire (What information, if any, did the suspect volunteer—At the scene? In patrol car? At headquarters?)

_____   VI. HOW
  A. How were the acts performed?
  B. Description of the scene, surrounding area and environment
  C. Description of the victim(s)
  D. Description of the suspect(s)
  E. How was entry gained? Exit?
  F. How was the property touched, moved, damaged, or destroyed?
  G. How was the property marked? Noting particularly:
    1. Type;
    2. Make;
    3. Model;
    4. Serial No.;
    5. Identification No.;
    6. Unique marks;
    7. Other

    H.   Unusual acts; unique MO

    I.   Associations of accomplices, co-conspirators, witnesses, etc.

    J.   How were any vehicles utilized?

    K.   How was the arrest effected? Noting particularly:
—The persons present, the suspect's actions immediately preceding the arrest, the necessary use of any force, the observation of any visible injuries on the suspect prior, and unrelated, to any police contact, etc.

___ VII. ANY NECESSARY ADDITIONS

    A. _____

    B. _____

    C. _____

    D. _____

    E. _____

    F. _____

    G. _____

    H. _____

Record All Relevant Facts and Strive for Accuracy

Naturally, if you have made an outline first, you should have all the relevant facts at your finger tips. Relevant facts, when incorporated into your report, generally become part and parcel of the relevant evidence which may be presented at a later legal proceeding.

How do you know when a fact (or item of evidence) is relevant? Generally, so long as the evidence has "any tendency to make the existence of any fact that is of consequence to the determination of the action more probable or less probable than it would be without the evidence,"[1] it is relevant. If you are not sure if a particular fact is a "relevant fact," that is, one which may be of consequence and make the existence of something more or less probable, include it anyway. If reasonable minds could differ over whether or not a particular fact is a relevant fact, chances are, that fact *is* relevant, and should be included. The inclusion of too much factually correct information (assuming your actions were proper) will not hurt you in future legal proceedings; however, leaving out important facts will indeed come back to haunt you.

Avoid legal conclusions

There is a clear-cut difference between a statement of a legal conclusion and a statement of fact. The following is illustrative:

---

1. *Fe(d)R.Evi(d)* 401.

Facts	Legal Conclusion
The motorist drove his car at a rate of speed significantly faster than the cars around him. In addition, he crossed over the center double yellow line three times, and each time caused the oncoming traffic to swerve around him.	The motorist drove *erratically and recklessly*.
I approached the driver's side of the vehicle and asked the driver to exhibit his license, registration and insurance. As I looked inside the passenger compartment, I observed a rolled marijuana cigarette in the opened ashtray.	I observed a rolled marijuana cigarette in *plain view*.
I observed both suspects sitting in the rear of the vehicle, handing back and forth a plastic wrapper which contained a white powder.	I observed *suspicious behavior*.
As I continued watching, I observed the suspect seated in the driver's side rear seat bring the plastic wrapper up to his nose and then sniff the white powder into his nose. I then confronted the individual and placed him under arrest.	I placed the suspect under arrest as soon as I had *probable cause*.
As I attempted to place the suspect in handcuffs, another subject quickly approached, grabbed my left hand, and attempted to wrestle the handcuffs away from me.	The subject *obstructed the lawful performance of my official duty*

Facts	Legal Conclusion
I began handcuffing the suspect after I informed him that he was under arrest. As soon as I touched the suspect's left hand, he quickly and forcefully turned around, pushed me away, and fled on foot.	The suspect *resisted arrest.*

As a general rule, it is the officer's job merely to convey his or her knowledge of the facts. Once the officer relates the facts, it is the job of the court to assess those facts and then pronounce the legal conclusion.

When an officer prepares an affidavit for a search warrant, he naturally does not request the particular search merely because he has "probable cause." Rather, he details the facts and circumstances which give rise to his probable cause. This provides a neutral and detached magistrate or judge with the necessary information to make an independent determination as to whether the warrant should issue. Mere legal conclusions such as: "...I have adequate grounds to suspect..."; or "I would request that a warrant should issue because I have probable cause to believe..." would never support the issuance of a search warrant within the meaning of our Constitution.

By analogy, the assertion of such legal conclusions in your report would not permit a "neutral and detached" reader to make an independent determination as to whether or not your actions—in light of the facts and surrounding circumstances—were proper. This is because *you have not stated what the facts and surrounding circumstances are;* a practice which can only serve to detract from the quality and strength of the government's case against the defendant; and it may also assist the defense attorney in his process of impeaching (or attacking) your credibility when you are called upon to take the witness stand and testify against his client. The impeachment will generally focus not only upon the veracity of your information but upon your basis of knowledge of the event, your ability and opportunity to have perceived the event, your ability to remember the event, and whether your actions were lawful and reasonable.

Significantly, in warrantless search and warrantless arrest situations, the Incident or Operations Report becomes the functional equivalent of an affidavit, and perhaps in some respects more critical than an affidavit. Whenever an officer conducts a search or seizure without a warrant, the procedure is considered presumptively unlawful. It then becomes the government's burden to establish that the search or seizure comes within one of the recognized exceptions to the written warrant requirement. If the relevant facts and circumstances which constitutionally justify the warrantless procedure are missing from the officer's report, the likelihood that the prosecution will not meet its burden is great. If the prosecution cannot meet its burden due to the deficient law enforcement reporting, the inescapable result, of course, is the needless suppression of the most probative evidence of the defendant's guilt.

Fully document sources of information

One of the most valuable assets in the law-enforcement battle against crime is the police informant. In fact, over the course of time, the proper utilization of information imparted by informants has led the courts to "consistently accept[] the use of informants in the discovery of evidence of a crime as a legitimate investigatory procedure consistent with the Constitution."[2]

Generally, informants are classified into three distinct types: *criminal informants, citizen informants,* and *anonymous tips.* The "type" of informant becomes important when a determination must be made as to whether the information imparted provides a sufficient constitutional justification for a particular police action. Moreover, knowledge of the type of informant the police are dealing with becomes critical when a determination must be made as to how much independent police investigation must be employed to verify or corroborate the information reported. As a general rule, the *less* reliable the information is, the more independent police corroboration is needed.

a.   *Criminal informants.* In the totality-of-the-circumstances analysis, the reliability of an informant's hearsay information, along with the informant's credibility, remains a relevant inquiry. In fact, one of the hallmarks of the competent criminal investigator is the ability to clearly and thoroughly document in an appropriate report not only the credibility of his or her confidential informant but the reliability of the information relayed and the informant's basis of knowledge. These items are "closely intertwined issues" which make up the "commonsense, practical question whether there is 'probable cause' to believe that contraband or evidence is located in a particular place."[3]

Perhaps the most common way reliability is established is by documenting the past use of the particular informant and the number of times the information imparted by that informant proved not only to be true and correct but also led to the arrest and successful prosecution of the subject of the information. A mere bare bones statement in a report (or an affidavit) that an informant is reliable and has proved to be reliable in the past is not enough. Officers should strive to include (1) how often the informant has been used; (2) the nature or character of the investiga-

---

2. *Arizona v. Fulminante,* 499 U.S. 279, 111 S.Ct. 1246, 1262-63 (1991) (Opinion of Rehnquist, C.J., dissenting in part).
3. *Illinois v. Gates,* 462 U.S. 213, 103 S.Ct. 2317, 2328 (1983).

tions in which the informant has previously supplied information (*e.g.,* narcotics, burglary, stolen property, arson, etc.); (3) how many times the information proved to be true and correct; (4) whether the information led to the arrest of the subject of the information; and (5) whether the subsequent prosecution led to conviction. Naturally, if any of the afore-mentioned indicators of reliability is absent or unknown, the report (or affidavit) would merely be silent in that regard.

Reliability may also be adequately established if, during the course of supplying information, the informant supplies his own name to the police and includes a "statement against his penal interest,"[4] for example, the case where the informant admits to buying narcotics on several occasions from a named individual. In such a case—where the informant admits to criminal conduct during the course of supplying information to the police—"[c]ommon sense in the important daily affairs of life would induce a prudent and disinterested observer to credit these statements. People do not lightly admit a crime and place critical evidence in the hands of the police in the form of their own admissions."[5]

Further, reliability may be enhanced if the informant provides the police with such information with the hope of changing his or her criminal ways. In this respect, it has been stated: "We are in a time when cocaine addiction is on the verge of epidemic proportion, and the public is extensively aware of the devastation created by it. Consequently, when a cocaine user voluntarily turns in his supplier to the police in the hope of shaking his reliance on the drug, and in doing so admits to his own criminal conduct, *such evidence sharply increases the degree of reliability* needed for the issuance of a search warrant."[6]

The informant's basis of knowledge may be established by documenting, in as much detail as possible, the informant's personal observations. This establishes how (and *when*) the informant came by his or her information, and demonstrates precisely what the informant personally saw, heard, smelled, tasted or touched. Persuasive in this regard would be details of the physical appearance of the target residence, exactly where in the residence the subject keeps or conceals the evidence or contraband, what the evidence or contraband looked like, how it was packaged, the name and detailed physical description of the subject and others who may also live at or occasion the target premises, and so on. This type and degree of detail not only fortifies the reliability of the information supplied but constitutes a material consideration in the totality-of-the-circumstances analysis.

The final ingredient in the totality-of-the-circumstances approach calls for the independent corroboration of as many of the facts relayed by the informant as possible. If time permits, all the information relayed should be confirmed by independent investigation. In this respect, a deficiency

---

4. *United States v. Harris*, 403 U.S. 573, 583, 91 S.Ct. 2075, 2081-82 (1971).
5. *Harris* at 583, 91 S.Ct. at 2082.
6. *State v. Goldberg*, 214 N.J.Super 401, 519 A.2d 907 (1986). [Emphasis added.]

in any of the foregoing elements may be counterbalanced by the officer's independent investigation—the touchstone of the totality-of-the-circumstances approach.

b. *Citizen informants.* In marked contrast to the criminal informant, an ordinary citizen, regarded as a cooperative member of the general public, presumably has no ties or connections with criminality. There is, therefore, "an assumption grounded in common experience that such a person is motivated by factors that are consistent with law enforcement goals."[7] Consequently, "an individual of this kind may be regarded as trustworthy and information imparted by him to a [law enforcement officer] concerning a criminal event would not especially entail further exploration or verification of his personal credibility or reliability before appropriate * * * action is taken."[8] As the Supreme Court of Wisconsin put it:

> A different rationale exists for establishing the reliability of named "citizen-informers" as opposed to the traditional idea of unnamed police contacts or informers who usually themselves are criminals. Information supplied to officers by the traditional police informer is not given in the spirit of a concerned citizen, but often is given in exchange for some concession, payment, or simply out of revenge against the subject. The nature of these persons and the information which they supply convey a certain impression of unreliability, and it is proper to demand that some evidence of their credibility and reliability be shown. * * *

> However, an ordinary citizen who reports a crime which has been committed in his presence, or that a crime is being or will be committed, stands on much different ground than a police informer. He is a witness to criminal activity who acts with an intent to aid the police in law enforcement because of his concern for society or for his own safety. He does not expect any gain or concession in exchange for his information.[9]

Moreover, credibility may be further enhanced if the particular citizen is "more than the ordinary citizen," for example, fire fighters, first aid or ambulance squad members, security personnel and the like. These individuals, while not sworn law enforcement officers, are more involved and presumably more public spirited than the average citizen, and in and of themselves may be considered credible sources of information.

c. *Anonymous tips.* Of all the types of information acted upon by law enforcement, the anonymous tip requires the *most* independent verifica-

---

7. *State v. Davis*, 104 N.J. 490, 506, 517 A.2d 859 (1986).
8. *Davis* at 506.
9. *State v. Paszek*, 50 Wis.2d 619, 184 N.W. 2d 836, 842 (1971).

tion. By its very nature, the anonymous tip carries with it none of the traditional indicators of reliability or trustworthiness which may attach to information imparted by citizen informants or even criminal informants. Thus, to develop the reliability of information imparted by the anonymous tip, officers must engage in two critical procedures: (1) comprehensive detail development, and (2) independent verification.

First, the individual who takes the call or receives the information must elicit as much detail as possible from the informer. Comprehensive detail development is crucial; it demonstrates the anonymous informant's "basis of knowledge," and provides substance and meaning to the second procedure in the development of reliability. Naturally, the call-taker should not initially attempt to ascertain the caller's identity. It is all too often that the question, "What is your name?" is followed by the sound of a dial tone. Rather, the call-taker should try to ascertain as much detail as possible as to what *exactly* the caller has observed (or is presently observing), the physical description of the subject of the caller's observations, how far away the subject was (or is presently) from the caller, whether the caller is presently watching the subject and if not, how long ago the observations were made, the exact location of the subject, whether there were or presently are any other people or vehicles in the area, and whether the caller would stay on the line while officers are dispatched. Once the call-taker has elicited as much detail as possible from the caller, the call-taker may then consider asking more "dangerous" questions, such as, "Are you a resident of the neighborhood?" "Do you live next to where these things are taking place?" "Where do you live?" "What is your name?"

The second step requires independent investigation directed at confirming or verifying each of the facts related in the anonymous tip. It is this independent corroboration which provides a foundation for a reviewing court to conclude that a substantial basis exists for crediting the hearsay information imparted by the anonymous tip. Significantly, as the officer proceeds to corroborate each of the details of the tip, it becomes increasingly evident that " [b]ecause [the] informant is right about some things, he is more probably right about other facts[.]"[10] Once an officer has personally verified every possible facet of the information contained in the tip, reasonable grounds may then exist to believe that the remaining unverified bit of information—that a criminal offense is occurring, or has occurred—is likewise true.[11] As the United States Supreme Court has stated, "such tips, particularly when supplemented by independent [law enforcement] investigation, frequently contribute to the solution of otherwise 'perfect crimes.' "[12]

---

10. *Illinois v. Gates*, 103 *S.Ct.* at 2335.
11. *Draper v. United States*, 358 *U.S.* 307, 79 *S.Ct.* 329 (1959).
12. *Gates* at 2332.

Avoid shorthand expressions

Law enforcement officers, and attorneys and doctors for that matter, love shorthand expressions. Why say a lot when you can say it all in just a couple of words? In law enforcement reporting, however, the use of shorthand expressions is not only inappropriate, it may even come back to haunt you. While the use of these words may make report writing faster and easier, they are a poor replacement for the factual detail which they circumvent. Moreover, it is all too easy for a defense attorney to attack the credibility of an officer who uses words of this nature.

Facts	Improper Use of Shorthand Expressions
When we arrived at the station, Mr. Jones began yelling and cursing. As soon as I opened the rear door of the patrol car, he spit in my face. He then refused to get out of the car.	When we arrived at the station, Mr. Jones became *belligerent* and *uncooperative*.
The suspect was arrested for violating the criminal statute titled, "Wandering, Remaining or Prowling in a Public Place for the Purpose of Obtaining or Distributing a Controlled Dangerous Substance."	The suspect was arrested for "Loitering in a Drug Zone."[13]
As I spoke with the suspect, I noticed that his hands were trembling. As he spoke, his lip quivered and his voice fluttered. Beads of sweat started to accumulate on his brow.	The suspect exhibited *extreme nervousness*.
The suspect then quickly reached into the inside pocket of his jacket with his left hand and attempted to grab an object of some kind.	The suspect then made a *furtive gesture*.

13. This improper shorthand expression has actually led to the unlawful arrest of persons who were simply "loitering" in a high drug-trafficking area—conduct that is not unlawful. See *Kolender v. Lawson*, 461 *U.S.* 352, 103 *S.Ct.* 1855 (1983); *Papachristou v. City of Jacksonville*, 405 *U.S.* 156, 92 *S.Ct.* 839 (1972).

Facts	Improper Use of Shorthand Expressions
I immediately reached out, held the suspect's hand in place and conducted a protective frisk. When I patted the breast area of his jacket, I touched an object that clearly felt like a gun. Immediately thereafter, the suspect quickly pulled away from my grasp, raised his hands, clenched his fists and assumed a fighting stance. As soon as he began to throw his first punch, I grabbed his arm, turned him around, applied handcuffs and informed him that he was under arrest.	After the suspect acted *suspiciously*, I *searched* him. When I felt the gun in his pocket, he started to get *violent. I then subdued* him by *neutralizing* his hands, and brought him in.
As I approached the suspect vehicle, the front passenger bent over and motioned to his right in what looked like an attempt to either reach for something or hide something. As he did this, his head disappeared from view for about two seconds and then reappeared.	The passenger made a *furtive gesture*.
I observed the motorist drive his car for two miles. During this time, he weaved in and out of his lane of traffic five times. In addition, when he weaved to the right, the car entered the shoulder of the road and the two passenger-side tires creased the grass strip which is adjacent to the shoulder of the road. I then activated my overhead lights and directed the motorist to stop.	I stopped the motorist for a *motor vehicle violation*.

Avoid questionable inferences

Unless you are clairvoyant, and can qualify as such in court, avoid drawing inferences as to what a person may have seen, heard, felt, or believed; or what a person may have been attempting to do or not to do on a particular occasion. While it is very natural to draw such inferences from an individual's conduct, many times those inferences are wrong, or at least questionable. Your job is simply to objectively describe the individual's conduct. Let the inferences or factual conclusions be drawn by the judge or jury.

Facts	Questionable Inferences
As I turned the corner, I saw the subject inserting a crowbar into the front door jam of the ABC Liquor Store.	As I turned the corner, I saw the subject attempting to break into the ABC Liquor Store.
At the time, I was in full uniform. As I walked closer to where the subject stood, he quickly turned and looked directly at me. As his eyes made contact with mine, his head jerked back suddenly. He then immediately dropped the crowbar, and ran.	I startled the subject as I walked closer to where he stood. As soon as he saw the police presence, he ran.
At the station, I asked the motorist for his name, address, date of birth and other biographical information. He responded with several slurred sounds, but did not answer any of the questions.	At the station, I asked the motorist for his name, address, date of birth, and other biographical information. He was so drunk, he could not respond.
I called out to the woman as she climbed onto the tenth-floor window ledge, but she did not answer.	I called out to the woman as she was about to commit suicide, but she couldn't hear me.

Facts	Questionable Inferences
The motorist told me that he did not see the other car prior to the collision because a large truck had obstructed his view.	The motorist did not see the other car prior to the collision because a large truck obstructed his view.

Never cite cases in your report

Unless you want to be cross-examined for hours concerning not only how knowledgeable you are of the case you cited but also on the extent of your knowledge of any and all cases that have been handed down which also address the particular subject, it may be a better idea to leave the law to the lawyers.

Be accurate

Note the exact times and places of significant events, and whenever possible, immediately document the notations in your field notebook. Events and items of significance may include, but not be limited to:

• The exact time you were dispatched to the scene (or observed the incident), and the exact time you departed from the scene;

• The exact location of the incident, or crime scene;

• The exact location where, and the time when, victims, suspects and witnesses were located, specifically noting their correct names, addresses, places of employment, telephone numbers or numbers of persons who could contact them for you (or the investigator) at some point in the future. Also make note of any comments or statements made by witnesses or victims, and any admissions offered by suspects, particularly noting the time when made;[14]

---

14. A common defense attorney cross-examination tactic is the focus upon a common or repeated time in an officer's report. For example, many officers will receive the time from the communications dispatcher upon their arrival at the scene or upon the initiation of a motor vehicle stop. It is a very dangerous practice to utilize that time as *the* time for *everything* that occurs thereafter. If after the initial time is received significant events occur, such as the receipt of a consent to search, an arrest, the administration of *Miranda* warnings, a suspect's request for a lawyer, a verbal admission or confession by the suspect, and the like, an officer should document the exact time of each particular event; and logic dictates that those times must invariably be different from the initial time provided by the dispatcher. One need only imagine the havoc which a good defense attorney could cause in cross-examination, questioning how any officer could possibly accomplish all those things at *one specific point in time*. It is also critical to note that any admission or statement made by the defendant *must* be formally documented and turned over to the prosecutor (and to the defense) in discovery. If not, the statement or admission will, in most states, be inadmissible at trial.

• The exact location of any property recovered or evidence seized;

• The exact times and places of, and environmental factors surrounding, arrests and eyewitness identifications;

• The exact appearance of *death scenes*. When responding to a death scene, suspicious or not:

> • Particularly note the exact location and position of the body and indicate if the body is moved *in any way* by the responding emergency medical team (or anyone else);

> • Note the surrounding environment: lights on or off, appliances on or off, whether the body was found lying by the window in the sunlight or near any artificial heat; atmosphere (dry or wet), and temperature (try to estimate in degrees);

> • Note any medication present, either near the body, in the medicine cabinet, etc., whether the pill bottles are empty, full, etc.; note the doctor's name on the bottles (this indicates that this may be an "attended" death); note the date of the prescription and whether it is in the name of the deceased; and

> • Note the exact time of death pronouncement and the identity of the medical person pronouncing.

(In all such cases, if something seems out of place or "suspicious," *indicate exactly why*.)

Bear in mind that if the above listed events are not recorded accurately, the misstatements or misdescriptions will serve only to detract from the quality and strength of the government's case, and at the same time diminish your credibility as a professional in the field and as a witness at a future legal proceeding.

Never, never lie in your report

Lying *will* come back to haunt you. It will instantly destroy your integrity; it can devastate your career; and it may even lead to criminal charges.

Don't rely on your memory, and don't fall into the trap of believing that you will remember a particular fact so you don't have to write it down. Knowing exactly what happened immediately after the event is one thing; remembering exactly what happened six months or a year later is entirely another. Even if you have a good memory, many months can pass from the time of the incident to the time you must testify about the incident. These intervening days, weeks, months, and in some cases, years include many other contacts, interviews, investigations and arrests. For example, if you average four arrests per week, and eleven months pass before the time of your trial testimony concerning the eleven-month old arrest, that means you have since made 176 arrests. How many contacts, interviews, investigations, and written reports is that? Those intervening events, as a matter of common sense, must tend to cloud, confuse or distort your memory of the earlier case.

As a result, if all the relevant or necessary facts are recorded immediately after they are perceived, the problem of insufficient recollection will be alleviated; additionally, the problem of inaccurate statements of times, locations, positions (of people or property) or descriptions should be eliminated. Thus, the commandment within the Commandment:

> *When you write your report, you must assume that you will recall absolutely nothing about the case at a point six months or a year from now, when you will be called upon to testify from that report.*

When you proceed with this assumption, and you accurately and completely "recreate the scene on paper," all that is thereafter necessary for trial preparation is the process of reviewing your report. Moreover, this practice will permit anyone reading your report (persons with no other knowledge of the event other than your report) to not only be able to easily and quickly acquaint themselves with the circumstances giving rise to the report, but to relive those events and circumstances in the same light in which you perceived or learned about them. Consequently, you will have recorded all the relevant facts comprehensively and accurately, thereby producing a finished product that invariably includes the "specific facts and circumstances" which, in addition to establishing probable cause, become an integral part of the evidence which will ultimately convict the accused.

Finally, this practice will serve to adequately refresh your recollection as to the exact sequence of events which gave rise to your report and all the details necessary to protect yourself from (destructive) cross-examination. Significantly, the practice of leaving important facts out of your original report will enable the defense attorney to easily impeach your testimony on the witness stand and credibility as a law enforcement officer. For example, a common defense attorney tactic is to try to make the Incident or Operations Report seem so much more important than the officer's testimony that any statement by the officer on the witness stand which contradicts, is inconsistent with, or materially supplements the written report immediately appears to be a recent fabrication. Consider the following example:

Q. Now officer, you were taught in the police academy to always take field notes, were you not?

A. We were taught to take field notes whenever the situation reasonably permits the taking of notes.

Q. "Officer, you testified on direct that you have been formally instructed at the training academy, correct?"

A. "Yes."

Q. "And part of that training covered report writing, isn't that so?"

A. "Yes."

Q. "And isn't it true that you were taught that your official report is a very important document?"

A. "Yes, very important."

Q. "You believe that it is an important document, don't you?"

A. "Yes, I do."

Q. "It's also true that you have been taught to include in your official report every fact that is important, isn't it?"

A. "Yes."

Q. "Officer, you made an official report in reference to this case, correct?"

A. "Correct."

Q. "This is your report?"

A. "Yes, it is."

Q. "And this is your signature at the bottom?"

A. "Yes, that's my signature."

Q. "You wrote this report the day after the incident?"

A. "No. I wrote it that very night."

Q. "That very night; and when you wrote the report, the facts, of course, were fresh in your mind, weren't they?"

A. "Yes, they were."

Q. "And at the time you made out your report, you believed it was true and correct?"

A. "Yes."

Q. "And of course you followed your training and included all the important facts in this report, didn't you?"

A. "Yes, I did."

Q. "You still believe your report is true and correct, don't you?"

A. "Yes, I do."

Q. "Well, officer, do you remember earlier when you testified to the fact that a second bystander informed you that my client was selling narcotics out of a limousine?"

A. "Yes."

Q. "Did you consider that important?"

A. "Of course."

Q. "Then, officer, could you tell us why that fact, that you just testified as being important, was not in your official report?"

A. [Here, whatever the officer says does not matter. The credibility of the report, along with the officer's testimony, in the eyes of the court, is severely damaged.]

Q. "You didn't think it was important then, but you think it is important now?"

A. [Now the officer is placed in a defensive and difficult position; the judge or jury must now try to decide which is correct, the officer's official report or the testimony which was just presented...or neither.]

Notes

Always Remain Objective

There is a clear-cut difference between *subjective* and *objective* writing. *Subjective* writing expresses the writer's personal feelings or emotions, opinions, biases or prejudices, and does so generally without regard to verifiable facts and evidence. *Objective* writing records the facts and circumstances without reference to the writer's personal feelings of the event; without emotion; and most importantly, without any implications of bias or prejudice.

For example, an objective, written exam is one given in the form of either a. multiple choice questions, b. fill-in-the-blank sentences, c. matching concepts or terms with explanations, and other similar forms which do not permit you to voice your views or opinions on the particular subject. Exams of this nature only permit you to "give the facts," uncolored by any personal feelings, opinions or critiques; and naturally, these facts are easily and completely verifiable. If for some reason such facts cannot be verified, the exam question is improper and can usually be successfully contested.

As a general rule, virtually all courts will analyze an officer's conduct not from his or her subjective state of mind—not from his or her personal motives or desires—but from an objective viewpoint, questioning whether, in light of all the circumstances, the officer's conduct was *objectively* reasonable. In this respect, the United States Supreme Court has emphasized that "evenhanded law enforcement is best achieved by the application of objective standards of conduct, rather than standards that depend upon the subjective state of mind of the officer."[1] As a result, any judicial inquiry into a law enforcement officer's conduct will rely not on

---

1. *Horton v. California*, 496 U.S. 128, 110 S.Ct. 2301, 2308-2309 (1990).

the officer's own subjective appraisal of a particular event, but upon a detached, neutral and objective evaluation of that event and the reasonableness of the officer's actions.[2] Those actions, of course, must be properly documented in an objective writing form, and the facts which are related must "be capable of measurement against an objective standard."[3]

This "objective mode of discourse," that is, this "objective tone of writing," should, as a general rule, be used in any official law enforcement reporting. Never permit your personal feelings, biases or prejudices to bleed through your writing onto the reader's hands. If you do, you have entered the world of subjectivity, and, the subjective mode is not appropriate for official law-enforcement communications; it is considerably less verifiable; it invites argument; and, interestingly enough, it lays down a welcome mat for defense attorneys to visit their impeaching, cross-examination tactics upon your trial testimony.

Leave all the literary criticisms, critiques and opinions of law enforcement events to the commentators in the field and the editorial page of the local tabloid. Your official report is not the place to editorialize. It is your job merely to accurately record the facts and circumstances surrounding the particular incident or event, and to do so in a completely objective manner.

As with many general rules, the rule of objectivity has a few exceptions. One exception may be found in the events leading to a protective frisk. If, during the course of a *Terry* stop, you develop reasonable grounds to fear for your safety, a pat-down of the subject's outer clothing is the next appropriate procedure. It is also perfectly appropriate to include in your formal report that the subject's actions caused you to "fear for your safety." Although this statement is subjective in nature, it is nonetheless proper for inclusion. It is, however, essential to include the specific facts and circumstances that caused you to "fear for your safety."

A second exception, closely related to the first, covers the circumstances surrounding the drawing of your service weapon, and your justification for doing so. Part of your justification may be subjective, for example: "The subject looked like he was reaching for a weapon." This statement is important, for it shows your state of mind at the time. So long as you detail in your report the facts and circumstances that caused you to believe the subject was reaching for a weapon, the subjective statement demon-

---

2. In *Scott v. United States*, 436 U.S. 128, 137, 98 S.Ct. 1717, 1723 (1978), the United States Supreme Court explained that under the Fourth Amendment, a law enforcement officer's subjective motives or desires are irrelevant. Rather, the Court ruled that the Fourth Amendment requires "an objective assessment of an officer's actions in light of the facts and circumstances known to him" at the time the actions were taken. According to the Court, the assessment is accomplished without regard to the underlying intent or motivation of the officers involved. Moreover, the fact that a law enforcement officer "does not have the state of mind hypothecated by the reasons which provide the legal justification for the officer's action does not invalidate the action taken as long as the circumstances, *viewed objectively*, justify that action." *I(d)* at 138, 98 S.Ct. at 1723. [Emphasis added.] *See also Massachusetts v. Painten*, 389 U.S. 560, 565, 88 S.Ct. 660, 662 (1968) ("sending state and federal courts on an expedition into the minds of police officers would produce a grave and fruitless misallocation of judicial resources") (White, J., dissenting).
3. *Delaware v. Prouse*, 440 U.S. 648, 654, 99 S.Ct. 1391, 1396 (1979).

strating your state of mind at the time is proper for your formal report.

Another exception deals with the recognition of certain contraband. For example, if, during a motor vehicle stop, you notice a plastic bag containing a white powdery substance located on the vehicle's console, and a triple-beam scale resting on the back seat, you may reasonably conclude that the substance is cocaine. Under these circumstances, there is nothing wrong with including a statement in your report that, based on your training and experience, you believed the substance was cocaine, or that you believed the triple-beam scale was related paraphernalia. Again, the details leading up to your subjective statement must be set forth in your report.

Certainly, there are other exceptions. As a rule of thumb, whenever it becomes necessary to draw a conclusion in your report, or include a subjective statement demonstrating your state of mind, be sure to also detail the facts and circumstances supporting your conclusion or statement. This gives the reader the opportunity to draw his or her own conclusions, and assess whether your conclusions were reasonable.

Notes

Strive for Clarity and Readability

Clarity and readability will include, but not be limited to:

a. One officer per report;
b. The proper use of words;
c. The use of words you understand and are comfortable using;
d. Correct spelling;
e. Proper punctuation;
f. Clear structure; and
g. The absence of cross-outs or white-outs, and legible hand-writing (typed reports preferred).

One officer per report

The easiest way to stress this requirement is through the following example.

> Officer Heer and Officer Thare responded to a call of a burglary in progress. One report was submitted, signed at the bottom by both officers. Here is how the report began:

"The undersigned responded to the above location at the above time and date answering a call of a burglary in progress. Upon arrival, I assumed a position at the front door while my partner covered the rear.* * * "

/s/ Officer Heer / Officer Thare

The problem: We do not know which officer is in the rear—whether "my partner" is either Heer or Thare!

The proper use of words

Language experts tend to agree that English, among all the languages in the world, is probably one of the most, if not *the most* difficult language to master. However, a mastery of all of the intricacies of the English language is not necessary. All that is necessary is a "handle on the mechanics of the language"; that is, merely being in possession of those skills which permit you to put words, phrases, sentences and paragraphs together to form a clear, precise and readily understandable message.

As a general rule, choose the word which most precisely explains the event or describes the person or object under consideration. For example, when describing the events of an assault:

Bad: The suspect punched the victim's lights out.

Better: The suspect punched the victim in the face, causing her to lose consciousness.

Or when describing a minor motor vehicle accident involving no damage:

Bad: Vehicle A crashed into vehicle B.

Better: Vehicle A's front bumper lightly tapped vehicle B's rear bumper.

Or when referring to law enforcement officer responses:

Bad: When my sergeant saw that my holster was unsnapped, she shrieked: "Square-up your service revolver!" (Law enforcement officers are professionals; no matter how exciting the event, they do not "shriek.")

Better: When my sergeant saw that my holster was unsnapped, she ordered: "Square-up your service revolver!"

In the proper circumstances, however, that word could be appropriate:

• As soon as the truck ran over the young child, a woman shrieked: "That's my baby!"

Words that are often confused

Affect / Effect

Affect is usually used as a verb meaning "to influence," to change," or "to assume." In psychology, *affect* is used as a noun to refer to feelings or emotions. Thus, use of *affect* as a noun is very limited.

> • Officer Brown's *affect* was very disturbed after the shooting. (as a noun)
> • The shooting did not *affect* Officer Jones. (as a verb)

Effect, when used as a noun, refers to the result, outcome or impression of something. As a verb, *effect* is used to cause or bring about something:

> • If you do not wear your body armor, the *effect* could be disastrous. (as a noun)
> • The commander tried to *effect* a change in the officer's behavior. (as a verb)

If you want to use a noun, use *effect*, unless you are referring to a person's emotions or psychological state.

> • Dangerous pursuits have a bad *effect* on many officers.
> • My words of encouragement didn't have the *effect* I thought it would.

On the other hand, if you want to use a verb, *affect* is the right choice in most cases. To be sure, substitute the words *cause* or *result* for *effect*, and *influence* or *change* for *affect*, then see which sounds better.

> • Too many reports to write *affects* [influences] my mood; it makes me agitated.
> • Too many reports to write *effected* [caused] the late hour at which I resumed patrol.
> • The court's decision in this case will not *affect* [change] our established procedures.
> • It will be a while before we can assess the full *effect* [result] of the new law.
> • It is essential that we *effect* [cause] an immediate increase in patrols in that area.

Biannual / Semiannual / Biennial

The words *biannual* and *semiannual* both mean the same thing: "occurring twice a year." *Biennial* means "occurring every two years." In law enforcement reporting, because of the possible confusion between *biannual* and *biennial*, use *semiannual* when you want to describe something that occurs *twice* a year. In addition, rather than using word *biennial*, simply report it as occurring *every two years*.

Biweekly / Bimonthly

Be careful when using these words. They do not mean the same thing. Moreover, to add to the confusion, *bimonthly* has two different meanings.

- The department pays *biweekly* [every two weeks]; we receive 26 checks a year.
- The department pays *bimonthly* [twice a month]; we receive 24 checks a year.

Caution:
- Your agency pays *bimonthly* [every two months]; you receive only 6 checks a year.

For clarity in writing, avoid the use of bimonthly. Write it simply as "twice a month" or "every two months."

Farther / Further

When referring to actual distance, use *farther* or *farthest*. Use *further* and *furthest* to mean longer, more, to a greater degree, or to a greater extent.

- The drive from the academy was *farther* than I expected. (meaning in actual distance)
- Bill threw the ball *farther* than Tom. (meaning a greater distance)
- I want to study this report *further*. (meaning longer or more in depth)
- This type of behavior can go no *further*. (meaning no longer)

First / Firstly, etc.

In law enforcement reporting, when enumerating, use the forms *first, second, third, etc*. **Do not use** *firstly, secondly, thirdly, etc.*

Gender / Sex

Use the word *gender* when referring to the social or cultural characteristics of males and females. Use the word *sex* when referring to biological characteristics.

- The investigation report identified the suspect's age and sex.
- The bias crime was committed on the basis of the victim's gender.

Good / Well

The word *good* is an adjective. The word *well* is an adverb.

- Officer Smith is a *good* shot. (adjective describing shot)
- You've trained Officer Smith *well*. (adverb describing trained)
- This is a *good* hamburger. (adjective describing hamburger)
- Trent received *good* grades at school (adjective describing grades)
- I can't taste the hamburger *well* because I have a cold. (adverb describing taste)
- I will do the job as *well* as I can. (adverb describing do)

Watch out for when these words are used with *linking verbs* or *action verbs*.

- You smell *good*. I'm glad you took a shower. (smell is a linking verb)
- Now that you took your cold medicine, you should be able to smell *well*. (smell is an action verb)
- You look *good*. (look is a linking verb)
- Look at this diagram *well*. (look is an action verb)

Note:
Good health and good spirits. To *feel well* means to be in good health. To *feel good* means to be in good spirits.

- Mary does not feel *well* today.
- The officers feel *good* about the new contract.

Have / Got

Strive to eliminate the use of the word *got*. Replace the phrase, *"I have got,"* with *"I have."*

Bad: I haven't *got* enough time to write this report.
Better: I don't *have* enough time to write this report.

Bad: I've *got* a lot of work to do tonight.
Better: I *have* a lot of work to do tonight.

Bad: I have really *got* to study this book for the exam.
Better: I really *have* to study this book for the exam.

Have / Of

Many report writers make the mistake of using the word *of* when *have* is the correct word.

Wrong: If she would *of* listened to me, this never would *of* happened.
Better: If she would *have* listened to me, this never would *have* happened.
Best: If she *had* listened to me, this never would *have* happened.

Wrong: I could *of* run through that exercise faster. I should *of* tried harder.
Right: I could *have* run through that exercise faster. I should *have* tried harder.

Wrong: Recruit Jones might *of* earned the highest grade in the academy class.
Right: Recruit Jones might *have* earned the highest grade in the academy class.

Irregardless / Regardless

Do not use *irregardless*. It is a nonstandard, inappropriate variation of the proper word, *regardless*.

Its / It's

The word *it's* is a contraction for *it is* or *it has*. Do not use it for anything else. The word *its* is possessive and shows that something owns or has something: its introduction, its conclusion. Even though we may write "the report's introduction" or "the report's conclusion" with an apostrophe; *its* already implies possession and doesn't need an apostrophe.

Wrong: *Its* amazing how often officers make this mistake.
Right: *It's* amazing how often officers make this mistake.

Wrong: *Its* time to go to work. *Its* been a long time since I drove to work.
Right: *It's* time to go to work. *It's* been a long time since I drove to work.

Wrong: *Its* amazing how often the department fails to honors *it's* fallen officers.
Right: *It's* amazing how often the department fails to honor *its* fallen officers.

Wrong: The report had a proper introduction, but *it's* conclusion needs work.
Right: The report had a proper introduction, but *its* conclusion needs work.

Lie / Lay

"Lie" is a *still* verb (also known as an "intransitive" verb). People *lie* on beds. Dogs *lie* on floors. The use of the word *lie* here suggests that the people and the dogs are very still. This verb does not require an object.

"Lay" is an *active* verb (also known as a "transitive" verb). A person picks up a dog and lays it on a blanket. A hen lays an egg. Use of the word "lay" suggests that someone or something is setting or placing something somewhere. This verb requires an object to complete its meaning.

Wrong: I will *lie* the gun on the table. (*TIP:* When in doubt, substitute the word *place* or *put*. If the sentence sounds right, the verb you want is *lay*. Since "*I will place the gun on the table*" sounds correct, the proper word is "*lay*.")
Right: I will *lay* the gun on the table.

Lie (to lie down): lie, lay, lain, lying.
- Today I lie in bed.
- Yesterday, I lay in bed.
- Many times, I have lain in bed.
- Yesterday, I was lying in bed all day.
- Lying in bed all day is not productive.

Lay (to place something or set something down): lay, laid, laying.
- Today, I lay the gun on the table.
- Yesterday, I laid the gun on the table.
- Many times, I have laid the gun on the table.
- Yesterday, I was laying the gun on the table when the sergeant entered the room.
- Laying guns on the table is against the rules of the department.

Lie (to tell a falsehood): lie, lied, lying.
- I know the suspect is lying.
- He told the police he had been lying in bed all night near his wife, who lay on the couch.
- Since his wife was out of town at the time, it is obvious that he is lying about where he's lain. I am sure that he has lied before.

Watch out for "lye." This is used to describe a strong alkaline solution—potassium hydroxide or sodium hydroxide.

Like / As

Like is a preposition used to compare one thing to another. It means "similar to" or "for example." It is generally used before nouns, noun phrases, and pronouns. *As* and *as if* are conjunctions used before clauses.

- *As* I previously mentioned…
NOT: Like I previous mentioned…

- It looks *as if* it is going to rain.
NOT: It looks *like* it is going to rain.
OK: It looks *like* rain.

- The suspect looks *as if* he is preparing to run.
- *As* in earlier encounters…
- I prepared diligently *as* I knew I should.
- Jim, *like* his predecessor, will need to deal with the problem.
- We need to recruit another person *like* you.
- This weapon looks *like* an AK-47.
- This smells more *like* marijuana than anything else.
- The suspect looks *like* his father.

Principle / Principal

The word *principle* can only be used as a noun. It is usually used to refer to a general law or basic rule. It also may be used to describe a faithful adherence to a code of ethics.

The word *principal* may be used as a noun or an adjective. As a noun, it may refer to the head of a school, the business owner or partner, or to a sum of money invested. As an adjective, *principal* means "the most important."

- The instructor presented a key *principle* of law enforcement.
- The captain is a person of *principle*.
- The *principal* of the high school called this morning.
- Officer Jones interviewed the *principal* of the law firm.
- This bank pays a very good return on my *principal*.
- This is my *principal* reason for applying.
- Let's go over the *principal* parts of the report.

Than / Then

The word *than* is a conjunction. Use it to link two parts of a sentence that are being compared to each other. *Then* is an adverb; it tells when something happened.

- My uniform is cleaner *than* your uniform.
- Officer Green finished his tour of duty, *then* drove home.
- I have more work tonight *than* you.
- I will finish the work I have, *then* I will go out with you.

Which / That

Use *that* as the first word of a phrase or clause that is essential for the sentence to make sense or to have its intended meaning. When the phrase or clause is not essential, use *which*.

Tip: If you can insert the words "by the way" and the sentence still has its intended meaning, use *which*.

- The gun *that* was used in the robbery was a .22 caliber revolver. (Here, the writer is not referring to just any gun. He/she is specifically referring to the gun that was used in the robbery. Therefore, the use of *that* is proper.)

- The .22 caliber revolver, *which* was used in the robbery, has the suspect's fingerprints on it. (In this case, the clause, "*which* was used in the robbery" is a by-the-way clause. The information is not essential; the information could be left out and the sentence would still make sense.)

When the information is essential, use *that* and don't use commas. When the information is not essential, use *which* and do use commas.

Wrong: The academy class, that I'm doing best in, is criminal law. (The clause, "that I'm doing best in" is essential for the sentence to make sense. Therefore, no commas should be used.)

Right: The academy class that I'm doing best in is criminal law.

Wrong: The suspect's right foot that is slightly larger than his left foot is the one that he used to kick the victim. (The clause, "that is slightly larger than his left foot" is a by-the-way phrase.)

Right: The suspect's right foot, *which* is slightly larger than his left foot, is the one that he used to kick the victim. (For by-the-way phrases, use *which* and insert commas.)

Who / That

Use *who* when referring to a person as an individual. Use *that* when referring to places, objects, animals, or a class or type of person.

> • He is the only recruit *who* can run the course in the allotted time.
> • Sam is the kind of student *that* can handle more work.
> • Sam is the student *who* scored the highest on the exam.
> • Bullet is the only dog *that* can locate the missing child.

Who / Whom

These pronouns may be used in asking questions, or may be used when referring to a noun or pronoun in the main clause of a sentence. Use *who* whenever *he, she, they, I,* or *we* could be substituted in the *who* clause. Use *whom* whenever *him, her, them, me,* or *us* could be substituted as the object of the verb or as the object of a preposition in the *whom* clause.

I wonder (who/whom) will be at the seminar today?
Try the substitutions; which sounds best?

> He will be at the seminar today. (sounds good)
> Him will be at the seminar today. (sounds bad)

Right: I wonder *who* will be at the seminar today?

Never argue with the guy (who/whom) is wearing the sergeant's stripes. Try the substitutions; which sounds best?

> He is wearing the sergeant's stripes. (sounds good)
> Him is wearing the sergeant's stripes. (sounds bad)

Right: Never argue with the guy who is wearing the sergeant's stripes.

With (who/whom) are you working today?
   Try the substitutions; which sounds best?

> I'm working with he. (sounds bad)
> I'm working with him. (sounds good)

Right: With *whom* are you working today?

- *Who* shall I say is calling? (I shall say *he* is calling.)
- The matter of *who* is responsible was not determined. (*He* is responsible.)
- *Whom* did you see today? (You did see *her* today.)
- It depends on *whom* they mean. (They mean *him*.)
- I need an officer *whom* I can trust. (I can trust *her*.)
- *Whom* do you want to handle the assignment? (Do you want *him* to handle the assignment?)

Whose / Who's

Use *whose* as the possessive form of *who*. The possessive form *whose* can mean either "of whom" or "of which." Thus, it can refer to a person or a thing. Use *who's* as a contraction meaning *who is* or *who has*.

- *Whose* gun is it? (It is *his*.)
- *Who's* the owner of that gun? (*He* is.)
- *Who's* had the most experience in that position? (*She* has.)
- *Whose* experience is best suited for that position? (*Her* experience is.)

Always avoid "police jargon." Besides sounding ridiculous and foolish, it is offending and non-professional. It also tends to violate THE SEVENTH COMMANDMENT.

Bad: The U/S then TCO'd the…and SOW'd the individual.
Better: I then took care of…and sent the individual on his way.

Bad: I booked the scumbag and then put him in the back for his three hots and a cot.
Better: I recorded the arrestee's identification   information in our police blotter (or booking log), and then placed him in our jail facility.

Bad: My snitch (or gink) helped me make this collar.
Better: My confidential informant provided the information for this arrest.

Bad: I then put the 2 Kees of nose candy in the evidence locker.
Better: I then placed the 2 kilograms of cocaine in the evidence locker.

Bad: Upon arrival at six bedrooms…they knew 5-0 had arrived.
Better: Upon arrival at Shore Terrace, North Carolina and Adriatic Avenues…the residents were aware of the police presence.

Bad: In order to keep the suspect under visual observation we maintained a surveillance over him.
Better: We watched the suspect.

Bad: Said officers desired to confront the aforesaid alleged perpetrator, and said officers proceeded to alight from said officers' patrol car.
Better: We got out of our patrol car and approached the suspect.

Bad: The undersigned officer and the aforesaid backup unit driven by Officer Smith effected a rendezvous at the above-described victim location.
Better: I met Officer Smith at 123 Main Street.

Bad: The shorts that the suspect was wearing were of the baggy type and were blue in color.
Better: The suspect wore baggy blue shorts.

Bad: Before being attacked, the victim's jacket was clean in appearance and blue in color.

Better: The victim's blue jacket was clean before the attack.

Bad: The aforesaid detective telephonically contacted him at his place of abode.

Better: Detective Jones phoned him at his home.

As you can see, the use of meaningless or imprecise words, fancy or formal expressions, police jargon or slang detracts from clear and concise reporting. The use of such language can confuse the reader, change the true meaning or perspective of an event, and it may also provide the defense with extra ammunition with which to impeach your credibility during cross-examination.

It is wrong to assume that the use of a lot of words will clarify a report. In fact, the opposite is true. Write in a straightforward, conversational tone, and keep in mind the KISS principle:

> Keep It Short and Simple.

The proper use of words also dictates that you should strive to avoid *"double talk."* If it's worth saying, it's worth saying once! Adding language which merely repeats what has already been said is a measure which detracts from the overall quality of the report.

Double Talk	**Say it Once**
The victim's comments were unforgettable. I will never forget them.	The victim's comments were unforgettable.
The witness woke up about midnight because of a loud crash that woke her up.	The witness woke up about midnight because of a loud crash.
Just before the assailant entered the diner, the victim was eating apple pie a la mode with ice cream.	Just before the assailant entered the diner, the victim was eating apple pie a la mode.
The victim repeated her story over again.	The victim repeated her story.

Effective Law Enforcement Report Writing

There are many examples of "double talk." In practice, many expressions we use in every day speech are redundant. Here are some examples:

EXAMPLES OF "DOUBLE TALK"
(REDUNDANT LANGUAGE)

advance warning	9:00 p.m. at night
100% unanimous	first time ever
6:00 a.m. in the morning	each and every one
separate out	repeat over again
important essentials	mix together
return again	so forth and so on
mutual cooperation	stalling for time
one and the same	rock back and forth
equally as important	other alternative
completely destroyed	may possibly
rise up	revert back
unexpected surprise	over and done with
usual custom	rarely ever
untrue lie	month of July
first start	extra additions
true fact	end result
right beside	small in size
blue in color	square in shape
most unique	really truly
satisfactory enough	sum total
few in number	the reason is because
circulate around	regular routine
final outcome	

Keep your report writing *crisp and clean*. Avoid the use of *unnecessary words*. These tend to distract your reader and, at times, confuse them.

Wordy	**Concise**
There are some officers who cannot help using a lot of unnecessary words and excessive verbiage when they write	Some officers cannot help being wordy when they write.

Wordy

It is my opinion that there are times in this day and age when I really feel strongly that we should give more assistance to those people who are currently homeless and without a place to live.

Concise

I feel strongly that we should assist the homeless more than we do.

The sergeant reviewed his officers' reports on a daily basis.

The sergeant reviewed his officers' reports daily.

The sergeant reviewed his officers' reports on a regular basis.

The sergeant reviewed his officers' reports regularly.

SOME MORE EXAMPLES

Wordy	Concise
at that point in time	then
ahead of schedule	early
I am in possession of	I have
in advance of	before
made an escape	escaped
it is my opinion that	I think
all of a sudden	suddenly
until such time as	until
in the event that	if
provided that	if
on the condition that	if
at a later date	later
due to the fact that	because
the reason why is that	because
owing to the fact that	since
had occasion to be	was
the undersigned	I
take into consideration	consider
did not pay attention to	ignored
as a matter of fact	in fact
in spite of the fact that	although
there is no doubt but that	no doubt
first of all	first
during the time that	while

Double Negatives

Be careful when using such "negatives" as: *no, none, nobody, nowhere, nothing, no one, never, not, can't, don't, wouldn't, hardly, scarcely, barely, rarely* and *unlike*. Double negatives actually cancel each other out.

Wrong: I <u>don't</u> have <u>no</u> ammunition for my duty gun. I <u>hardly</u> <u>never</u> run out of ammunition, but when I do, my embarrassment is <u>unlike</u> <u>none</u> other.

Right: I <u>don't</u> have <u>any</u> ammunition for my duty gun. I <u>hardly</u> <u>ever</u> run out of ammunition, but when I do, my embarrassment is <u>like</u> <u>none</u> other.

Wrong: I <u>haven't</u> seen <u>no</u> suspects in the area.
Right: I <u>haven't</u> seen <u>any</u> suspects in the area.

Wrong: I <u>don't</u> see <u>hardly</u> any reason to continue this conversation.
Right: I see <u>hardly</u> any reason to continue this conversation.

Wrong: I <u>didn't</u> see <u>no</u> witnesses. (This means I *did see* witnesses!)
Right: I <u>didn't</u> see any witnesses.

Odd: At <u>no</u> time did I know <u>nothing</u> on the exam.
Better: At all times I knew something on the exam.

Use words you understand

This begs the question: Why would anyone use a word they do not understand? Although the answer to this question is not always clear, many officers will nonetheless use words which are vaguely familiar, or words which, although having a "professional ring" to them, are highly inappropriate in the context to which they are put to use in the report. This often occurs when officers try to use "legal terms of art" to make their report sound more official or to impress the reader. For example: "I searched the trunk of the vehicle pursuant to my preponderant evidence indicating the requisite belief that...."

Thus, if you are not sure of the precise meaning of a word you are about to use, use a different one. Simplicity brings clarity. Do not strike a pose or write to amuse, entertain or impress. Remember, many people will be reading your report. Some of them are prosecutors and judges—people who are not often amused or impressed, but easily aggravated. Defense attorneys will, however, be amused by such a report. They will also use it against the prosecutor during pretrial hearings and the plea bargaining process. And they will most certainly use it against you during cross-examination.

For a listing of commonly misused words, please
refer to the Reference Section of this book
beginning on page 269.

Strive for accurate spelling

Proper spelling is critical for effective law enforcement report writing.
Spelling errors not only detract from the overall quality of a report but
also call into question the credibility of the writer.

For a listing of commonly misspelled words, please
refer to the Reference Section of this book
beginning on page 281.

Pay attention to your punctuation

The most extreme example of a punctuation problem is the two-page report which begins with a capital on the first page and ends with a period
at the bottom of the second. Give the reader a chance to catch his breath.
As a general rule, if *you* think that the sentence is too long, it probably
is.

The proper use of punctuation will enhance the report's clarity by:

(1) Preventing overreading;
(2) Providing the necessary breaks in thought; and
(3) Easing the reader's burden.

The improper use of punctuation not only detracts from the overall quality of a report, but it can adversely impact the intended message.

Punctuation types

Period (.)
A period ends a sentence that is not a question or an exclamation.

Question Mark (?)
A question mark ends a sentence or a clause that is asking a question.

- Who is that man?

Exclamation Point (!)
An exclamation point is used to provide emphasis (yelling) to an expression.

- The unknown man yelled, "Surprise!," immediately before he threw the pie at my face.

Colon (:)
A colon indicates that a list is going to follow.

- The teacher taught the following classes: math, science, algebra, art, and Spanish.

A colon is also used after words such as caution, wanted, or note.

- Caution: slippery floor
- Wanted: part-time secretary
- Note: We're finished.

Semicolon (;)
A semicolon is used to separate two clauses that are independent, yet continue the thought. Independent clauses are complete sentences. Note: A semicolon is stronger than a comma but slightly weaker than a period

- The man has no money left; he was gambling all night.
- His family is Jewish; they celebrate Chanukah but not Christmas.

A semicolon may also be used to separate elements when the various elements have commas within them.

- The teenager bought a small, blue car; four large, wide racing tires; and an expensive engine to install in the car.

In addition, use a semicolon before "conjunctive adverbs," such as how-ever, meanwhile, otherwise, besides, indeed, etc., when such words are used to show a relationship between two complete sentences.

> • You probably thought there were no more rules for semicolons; however, you were wrong.

Apostrophe (')
An apostrophe is used to indicate possession.

> • John's wallet is on the table.

An apostrophe indicating possession generally involves placing an apos-trophe followed by an "s," unless the subject is plural and ends with an "s." If the subject is plural and ends with an "s," the apostrophe merely follows the "s."

> • I have the boy's sneakers. [one boy]
> • I have the boys' sneakers. [more than one boy]

An apostrophe is also used to form a contraction.

> • She'll have to call me tomorrow. [She will / She'll]
> • Don't even try it. [Do not / Don't]

The exception for the apostrophe being used to indicate possession is the distinction between "it's" and "its." With respect to "it's," the apostro-phe is only used to form the contraction, "it is." The possessive form is merely, "its," without the apostrophe.

> • The car lost its traction. [possessive]
> • It's going to be hard to explain this. [It is / It's]

Comma (,)
A comma is used to indicate a pause in a statement.

> • If the noise continues, I will have to call the police.

Use a comma to provide for the natural pause in a statement. Commas are often used to replace "and" in a sentence. They are also used to pro-vide the appropriate context and meaning of a sentence.

> • The small, vicious dog bit the child. [comma replaced and]
> • I am so angry I could scream, Joe, so let's go. [w/o the comma before "Joe," the statement would have a totally different meaning]

Roots, prefixes, and suffixes

One of the best ways to improve your vocabulary is to read, read, and read some more. It is only through using and interacting with the English language that you will be able to develop any real mastery of it.

Another way to improve your vocabulary is to study and learn the significant "subparts" of words. Most words used in the English language today were not originally English. The words have been adopted from other languages, such as Latin and Greek. When improving you vocabulary, it is helpful to know some of the origins or "roots" of English words. It may then be possible to guess the meaning of an unknown word when you know the meaning of its roots. In addition, knowing prefixes and suffixes can further assist in the process.

Many English words consist of three parts: the *root*, a *prefix* and a *suffix*. The root is the part of the word that contains the basic meaning (definition) of the word. It is considered the "base element" of the word. A prefix is a word element that is placed in front of a root. A prefix changes the word's meaning or makes a new word. A suffix is a word element that is placed after the root. The suffix changes the word's meaning as well as its function (use). Prefixes and suffixes are called *affixes* because they are attached to a root.

Act, React, and Reaction

The root, *act* means "do" or "perform."
    (v.) to perform, behave;
    (n.) a performance, a thing done

• You act like a professional.

The prefix "re-" means "back" or "again"
Prefix + Root = react (literally meaning "do back")
    (v.) to act in response or opposition to something.

• How will he react when he learns of the result?

The suffix: "-ion" indicates that the word has
    become a noun
Prefix + Root + Suffix = reaction (literally meaning
    "something done back")
    (n.) a response to something; an opposing action.

• His reaction to the news was very professional.

Prefixes and suffixes were originally words themselves, but they are now groups of letters which are added to words or to roots to create new words. Prefixes [pre (before) + fix (fasten) = fasten before] are groups of letters placed before words or roots. Prefixes modify or extend the meanings of words and roots. Suffixes are groups of letters attached to the ends of roots, words, and word groups. Suffixes serve a grammatical function. A suffix can indicate what part of speech (noun, verb, adjective, adverb) to which the word belongs. Suffixes can also modify and extend meaning.

For a listing of roots, prefixes, suffixes, meanings, and examples, please refer to the Reference Section of this book beginning on page 287.

Correcting structure problems

(1) *Chronological order.* As a general rule, record your observations, actions, and all relevant events in chronological order, that is, record these items in the exact order of *time of occurrence*. This practice greatly assists the reader's understanding of the events recorded. Moreover, chronological order permits the reader to "watch" the events through your eyes and ears in the same time sequence those events came to your attention.

(2) *Use an active writing style.* Structure your sentences in the active voice whenever possible. Active voice portrays actions, events, or observations "happening now." In its simplest form, active writing would take on the following structure:

Subject — verb — object
Suspect — shot — victim.

Bad: The first shot was fired by the suspect.
Better: The suspect fired the first shot.

Bad: The victim was struck in the face by the suspect's fist.
Better: The suspect used his fist and struck the victim in the face.

Bad: The pedestrian was hurled over the railing by the impact of the boardwalk tram.
Better: The impact of the boardwalk tram hurled the pedestrian over the railing.

Bad: The officer did not give a satisfactory explanation of the shooting.

Better: The officer did not adequately explain the circumstances of the shooting.

Accordingly, active writing will not only save you time and space, but it will also enhance the clarity of your report by adding specificity to your style, force to your delivery, and precision to your descriptions.

(3) *The best beginning.* Never begin your report in the following way:

"On the above date and above time, the undersigned responded to the above location and spoke to the below named resident concerning damage to the above described premises."

This type of beginning annoys virtually all prosecutors and detectives or investigators, while at the same time unnecessarily increasing their reading burden. Rather, the better beginning might have been written as:

"On Wednesday, April 19, 2002, at approximately 6:40 p.m., I, Officer James Swift, was dispatched to 123 Main Street in reference to a 'malicious damage to property' call. Upon arrival, I spoke to the 123 Main Street property owner, who identified himself as:

John Jones
123 Main Street
Anywhere, U.S.A. 19122
Phone: (215) 787-1234
Business: ABC Lumber Co.
Bus. Phone: (215) 787-3456

Mr. Jones stated that…"

Try to begin your sentences with nouns—that is, names of persons, places, or things—or, pronouns.

Bad: After grabbing the woman's purse, the defendant threw her to the ground.

Better: Defendant grabbed the woman's purse and threw her to the ground.

While it may not be possible to start *every* sentence with a noun (or pronoun), most may be written that way. This style greatly enhances the writing's clarity and readability.

Another important thing to remember when beginning a report, or when beginning any sentence, is: Don't start a sentence with a numeral.

Wrong: 1,250 spectators viewed the assault.

Right: Twelve hundred and fifty spectators view the assault.

Right: There were 1,250 spectators who viewed the assault.

(4) *The problem with pronouns.* Pronouns substitute for nouns. Pronouns refer to persons, places, things, feelings and qualities—though not by name—and function as subjects, objects, etc. Without the use of pronouns, your writing would bog down in repetition. Pronoun examples include:

   i.   First Person Pronouns, used to refer to yourself:
        I, my, mine; we, our, ours

   ii. Second Person Pronouns, used to refer to those you are talking with:
        you, your, yours

   iii. Third Person Pronouns, used for whomever or whatever you are talking about:
        he, she, it; his, her, hers, its; him, her, the undersigned, it; they, theirs, them

Pronouns must "agree" with the nouns for which they are substituting. "Agreement" requires the pronoun to refer *clearly* to that noun and not to any other; and, as a general rule, the pronoun substitute refers to the noun immediately preceding it; if it doesn't, confusion is bound to result. For example, you cannot talk about a car in one sentence and substitute the pronoun, "they," for that car in the next sentence. "They" does not "agree" with car. Do not say "they" if you mean "it." If there is more than one car, naturally, "it" changes to "them."

iv. Some common problems:

1. The suspect pointed his gun and demanded the victim's wallet. He fled in a blue Camaro.

> Who fled? The way that is written, one must assume the victim fled.

2. The children called for help. He was having a seizure.

> Who was having a seizure? One of the children?

3. Patrol unit 4E pursued the speeding Corvette. They were intercepted at Arkansas and Atlantic Avenues.

> Who was intercepted? The occupants in the speeding Corvette (assuming there was more than one), or the officers in the patrol unit?

4. Car A, moving North on Georgia Avenue, crashed into Car B when it turned left at the northwest corner of Arctic and Georgia Avenues.

> Which car turned left? The way this is written, we must incorrectly assume Car B turned left.

The result in problem 4 is that the writer has changed a simple accident into a major court battle! He has altered the sequence of events, and has violated **THE EIGHTH COMMANDMENT** by incorrectly having the pronoun, "it," refer to the wrong car; it also indicates that Car B took the initiative. This not only removes us twice from the actual event, but provides the motorist in Car A with a defense he does not truly deserve. What to do? Repair the damage:

> Car A was traveling North on Georgia Avenue. Car A then made an illegal left turn onto Arctic Avenue and collided into Car B which, at the time, was traveling east on Arctic Avenue in a lawful manner.

(5) *Paragraph structure.* Pay attention to the way in which you structure your paragraphs. Basically, each paragraph should be limited to one idea, and the central statement of the paragraph should appear near the beginning, if not the first sentence. Clarity and unity of thought is then achieved by relating all other details of the paragraph to the central statement. If you would like an example, go back and read this paragraph again!

How long should the paragraph be? As a general rule, the paragraph in official law enforcement reporting should not exceed 100 words. Paragraphs running longer than 100 words not only cloud the writing's clarity, but diminish its readability. Additionally, large blocks of seemingly never-ending sentences have a monotonous appearance that intimidates the reader.

Accordingly, for Incident or Operations Reports, paragraphs should not exceed 100 words. In administrative reports or memoranda, due to their particular format, the average paragraph length should not exceed 65 words.

(6) *Number confusion.* As a general rule, write out numbers one through nine and use numerals for 10 and up. One exception, as explained earlier, is that a sentence should not begin with a numeral. Another exception permits the use of small numerals for sake of consistency.

Inconsistent: At the armory, we saw thirty-two semi-automatic handguns, 14 revolvers, twenty-seven shotguns, and 3 assault rifles.
Consistent: At the armory, we saw 32 semi-automatic handguns, 14 revolvers, 27 shotguns, and 3 assault rifles.

To avoid confusion in side-by-side numbers, consider the following:

Confusing: There were 16 6-foot recruits in the academy.
Clear: There were 16 six-foot recruits in the academy.
Also Clear: There were sixteen 6-foot recruits in the academy.

Yet another exception to the rule provides that the writer should use all numerals–even for the numbers 1 through 10 (as in this sentence)–when they have technical significance or need to stand out for quick comprehension. Use of this "all numeral" style is appropriate for use in tables, statistical material, and in expressions of dates (*June 5*), money ($8), clock time (*8 p.m.*), proportions and ratios (*a 10 to 1 shot*), academic grades (*96*), and percentages (*7%*). This exception also applies to abbreviations with symbols (*8 cm*, *9°F*), with numbers referred to as numbers (think of a number between 1 and 10), with highway designations (*U.S. Route 1*, *I-95*), periods of time (*a 6-month training period*), measurements (*packages over 3 pounds*), and page numbers (*page 3*).

When reporting "time," strive to present it in a clear, *easy to read* form.

Hard to Read: The recruit ran the course in three hours, twenty-eight minutes and five seconds.
Easy to Read: The recruit ran the course in 3 hours, 28 minutes, and 5 seconds.

Hard to Read: The shooting occurred at 10 o'clock in the evening.
Easy to Read: The shooting occurred at 10 p.m.

When entering denominations of money in a report, strive for *clarity and readability.*

Hard to Read: four dollars and thirty-six cents
Easy to Read: $4.36

Hard to Read: three million, seven hundred thousand dollars
Easy to Read: $3.7 million

Hard to Read: $300, 000, 000, 000
Easy to Read: $300 billion

Hard to Read: $0.47
Easy to Read: 47 cents

When using indefinite numbers and amounts, spell it out.

- several hundred students
- hundreds of inquiries
- a few thousand automobiles
- thousands of spectators
- a multimillion-dollar investment
- many millions of dollars
- a man in his late thirties
- packages of fifties and twenties

When using "ordinals" to indicate position or ranking, write them out if they contain only one word. Use numerals if the ordinal contains more than one word.

- Mary was the *first* officer to arrive at the scene; Bill was the *second.* (*Not 1st or 2nd*)
- Sam ranks *tenth* in his class and *twentieth* in the state. (*Not 10th or 20th*)
- Tom is ranked *32nd* in his class, and Frank is ranked *135th.* (*Not thirty-second or one hundred thirty-fifth*)

(7) *Structure signals.* The most important ingredients in the Incident or Operations Reports are the characters who play the major parts in the events or circumstances which give rise to the reports. Because of this, the writer should "signal" the reader as to the exact location of each of the character's description (whether that character is the victim, witness, or suspect), items of evidence, personal property, or real property. The following example demonstrates this technique.

"On Wednesday, April 1st, 2002, at approximately 6:40 p.m., I, Officer James Swift, was dispatched to 123 Main Street in reference to a 'malicious damage to property' call. Upon arrival, I spoke to the 123 Main Street property owner, who identified himself as:

> (Victim)
> John Jones
> 123 Main Street
> Anywhere, U.S.A. 19122
> Phone: (215) 787-1234
> Bus.: ABC Lumber Company
> Bus. Phone: (215) 787-3456

Mr. Jones stated that when he arrived home from his office at approximately 6:00 p.m., he found that his prize 'Rocky' statue, which normally stands upright in the middle of his lawn, was turned over, and Rocky's head was damaged beyond repair. Mr. Jones stated that his 'Rocky' was worth over $10,000, and gave me the purchase receipt (see attached property report)."

As can be readily seen, the indentation of the victim's name and other personal information not only serves as a quick index for "party-spotting"[1] but also eases the reader's burden by breaking up the continuous text. This indentation format, as a structure signal, should be used when describing:

i.   Victims,
ii.   Witnesses,
iii. Suspects,
iv.   Crime Scenes,
v.   Evidence,
vi.   Stolen (or recovered) property,
vii. Item lists (such as the one you are presently reading), and
viii. Any other similar items which readily lend themselves to the indentation format.

---

1. The indentation format is also an invaluable aid to an officer's courtroom testimony. This format quickly facilitates an officer's response to any question concerning the identity of witnesses, victims or suspects; it also eliminates any hesitation when answering any question concerning the location or description of evidence.

Write legibly, avoid cross-outs and white-outs, & strive for neatness

(1) *Legible Handwriting.* It should go without saying that your writing should be legible, that is, capable of being easily read or deciphered. Do not insult your reader's intelligence (remember **THE SECOND COMMANDMENT**) by asking them to figure out, sort out, unscramble or decode what you have written.

(2) *Avoid cross-outs or white-outs.* Never submit an official document—and your Incident, Operations, or Investigation Report is an official document—with cross-outs or white-outs. Major cross-outs or white-outs tend to suggest a credibility or accuracy problem in the report.

(3) *Strive for neatness.* As one police sergeant has stated: "How can you walk a beat if your shoes ain't neat?" The analogy to an officer's report should be immediately apparent.

Always Read Your Report Before Submitting It

Whenever you write a report, you should set it aside for three to five minutes before you read it for clarity. When it is too fresh in your mind, your mind's eye sees what you want it to see, not what's really there. In this respect, you are initially "word blind" to your own material. What you intended to include in your report doesn't always find its way to the paper. Therefore, you must put the report aside for a few minutes to give your brain a chance to digest what you have written. Then return to your report and read it in its entirety. You will be surprised how many things you'll find missing that you "thought" you wrote down.

Always write your report with the idea in mind that you are answering all possible questions with every sentence you put down. Ask: Does this make sense? Does it report what actually happened? Is it coherent? Will someone else understand this? Read each paragraph after you have written it down and ask: Could anyone— anyone who was not there at the scene—have a question about this particular fact or occurrence? Does this report adequately recreate the scene? If it does not, go back and review **THE SECOND COMMANDMENT.**

This practice, when combined with **THE SECOND COMMANDMENT,** will yield reports which are sharp and crisp, clear and coherent, and not only easily understood, but incapable of being misunderstood.

Notes

Preview
and Review

The heart of this Commandment is report review; and, it is of particular significance when the report is submitted to an investigator or detective. *Always, always insist on review.*

In more involved or more serious cases, *preview* the facts and circumstances of the case with the investigator or detective *before* you begin the process of drafting your report. This is of utmost importance when the case involves multiple officers, victims, witnesses or suspects. The "preview" will serve (just like your outline) as a completeness tool, and will guarantee consistency in the case. Inconsistencies in multi-officer, multi-party cases are a defense attorney's dream and a prosecutor's nightmare.

There may be times when a supervisor, for some reason, is unavailable to review the Incident or Operations Report before the investigating detective must draft the Investigation Report, and naturally, your Incident or Operations Report is a vital ingredient in that investigation. Don't hand the detective or investigator your report and disappear. Give him or her the opportunity to review what you have written—just in case you may have missed something in your report which that detective or investigator feels is important to the case.

The saying: "Two heads are better than one," most appropriately applies to the investigative or supervisory review of official reports. When the investigator (or supervisor) and the field officer put their heads together to double-check the contents of the Incident or Operations Report, the result is a report which is more consistent, more detailed, and much more effective; a report which displays a degree of professionalism which neither officer could possibly accomplish on his or her own.

Most important in this respect is the professionalism concept. Do not take any helpful or constructive criticisms to heart. They are never intended as a personal attack. As a professional in the field, you must recognize that any suggestions or criticisms offered serve not only to improve the government's case, but to further professionalize and enhance your ability to engage in *Effective Law Enforcement Report Writing*.

PART II
PRACTICE QUESTIONS
AND PROBLEMS

Succinct Writing is writing which is clearly expressed in few words; concise; characterized by brevity and clarity

Directions:

Items #1 – #15 consist of a series of excerpts from recently reviewed narrative reports. You plan to conduct roll call refresher training on Report Writing. You want to include in your training an exercise on writing succinctly, so you have taken examples from a number of poorly written reports to show what NOT to do. Using only the information given in the notes, select which statement—(a), (b), (c), or (d)—would MOST correctly and succinctly present the information originally found in the narrative.

GO ON TO THE NEXT PAGE.

1. I asked the subject being interviewed to provide her full name.
   She said, "Madonna."
   My partner was very aware of this interviewee and knew of the case.
   My partner informed me that the name "Madonna" was always used by this subject as an alias.

   (a) During questioning, the interviewee gave her name as Madonna. According to my partner, this was not the interviewee's real name.

   (b) When we questioned the interviewee, he provided her name as Madonna. According to my partner, the name was clearly one used as an alias by the interviewee.

   (c) Madonna gave me an alias name during interrogation. This was corroborated by my partner, who was quite familiar with the subject in this case.

   (d) I asked the interviewee her name and she responded, "Madonna." Later, my partner informed me that this name was very often utilized by this subject as an alias.

2. I saw four juveniles coming out of Wawa.
   Three of the juveniles carried backpacks.
   One of them carried a large radio.
   I could not determine if the radio was on at the time.

   (a) I observed four juveniles leaving; three carried backpacks, one had a radio which was not playing at the time.

   (b) I observed four juveniles leaving the Wawa store. Three carried backpacks and one carried a large radio.

   (c) I observed four juveniles come out of the Wawa store. Three carried backpacks, one had a large radio. I could not determine if the one with the radio had it turned on.

   (d) I observed four juveniles coming out of Wawa. Three had backpacks, the other had a large radio. A lot of noise in the area prevented my ability to determine if the radio was on.

GO ON TO THE NEXT PAGE.

3. I, the undersigned, along with Officer Collins, was detailed to investigate a warehouse burglary.
    Together, we drove over to the warehouse.
    At the time, the warehouse was closed tight and secure.

    (a) Our team was unable to complete this assigned burglary investigation as we found the warehouse closed.

    (b) Officer Collins and I, assigned to investigate a warehouse burglary, drove to the warehouse and found it closed and secure.

    (c) We investigated a warehouse burglary but were unable to pursue the investigation because the warehouse was closed.

    (d) Officer Collins and I drove to the warehouse of a burglary in progress, and were able to determine during the course of this investigation that the warehouse was secure.

4. Upon review of the officer's preliminary investigation report, I noted several problems.
    One was the failure to properly state the What, How, Who, Where, When, and Why.
    Other problems included several unprofessional erasures and the absence of a signature.
    This officer (Officer Tompkins) obviously needs to be sent to report-writing refresher training.

    (a) Upon review, I found numerous errors in the officer's report. I consider that the report indicates a failure of ability on this officer's part to write proper reports that needs training.

    (b) The problems in Officer Tompkins' report suggests the need for retraining.

    (c) My review of Officer Tompkins' preliminary investigation report revealed several report-writing problems, such as (1) too many erasures; (2) not completing the "Who, What, Where, When, Why and How" of the incident, and (3) failing to sign the report. I recommend this officer receive refresher training in writing proper reports.

    (d) A review of this officer's report revealed several unprofessional report writing errors which clearly impacted on this officer's credibility. The problems included not completing the "Who, What, Where, When, Why and How" of the incident, uncalled-for erasures and not signing the bottom of the report where the signature should appear. This officer should be given refreshment training in writing proper reports.

GO ON TO THE NEXT PAGE.

5. We investigated a "loud music" call.
    This is the first time we received a call from this address.
    At the location, we interviewed several neighbors.
    The neighbors were very angry.

    (a) Several neighbors were interviewed in relation to a first-time "loud music" complaint.

    (b) During the investigation of a first-time "loud music" call from this address, angry neighbors were seen loitering in the area.

    (c) Investigation of a new "loud music" call included the interviewing of neighbors.

    (d) During the investigation of a "loud music" call, the first such call from this address, we interviewed several angry neighbors.

6. My partner, Officer Blue, and I were called to Big Mart by store security.
    We drove to the store.
    A twelve-year-old boy was caught shoplifting.
    He left the store with a Gameboy. (Retail $70).
    Store alarm went off.

    (a) My partner and I were called by security to go to the shopping mall. The store alarm went off when a twelve-year-old boy left without paying for a Gameboy video game.

    (b) Store security called us to Big Mart because a twelve-year-old had stolen a Gameboy.

    (c) Officer Blue and I were called by a security official at Big Mart. Upon arrival at the store, we learned that a twelve-year-old boy was caught shoplifting. The boy had activated the store's alarm when he walked out with a Gameboy valued at $70.

    (d) A Gameboy worth $70 was shoplifted by a twelve-year-old young boy. My partner and I were called by store security. The store's security system was triggered by the twelve-year-old boy.

GO ON TO THE NEXT PAGE.

7. I received a phone call from a woman.
    She said her pocketbook was stolen from her house while she was gardening in the backyard.
    The front door was unlocked at the time of the theft.
    I went to 119 East 14th Street to investigate.

(a) I was called to 119 East 14th Street by a woman whose pocketbook was taken from her home. She stated that she had left the front door unlocked while she was in the backyard gardening.

(b) A woman called to report her pocketbook had been taken from her house while she was outside. She lived at 119 East 14th Street and had left the front door open at the time of the theft.

(c) I got a call from a woman who lived at 119 East 14th Street. She called to report that she had left her front door unlocked and that her pocketbook had probably been stolen while she was gardening nearby.

(d) After receiving a call from a very upset woman, I went to her house at 114 East 19th Street. She reported that she had gone out to her backyard to garden. When she came in her pocketbook was gone. She said she had not locked the front door.

GO ON TO THE NEXT PAGE.

8.   Officer Clark and I received a call of a complaint from the Metro Parking Garage attendant.
     The parking garage attendant complained that a belligerent man was refusing to pay his bill.
     He further stated that the man was blocking the exit to the garage right now.
     According to the attendant, the man was drunk at the time.

   (a) A belligerent drunk was refusing to pay his bill and leave so the parking lot attendant called me and my partner.

   (b) My partner and I were called about a nasty belligerent drunk man at a parking garage. He said he was refusing to pay his bill and that he was blocking the exit of the garage.

   (c) Officer Clark and I received a call from the Metro Parking Garage attendant. He complained of a drunk man who was very belligerent. He said that the man was refusing to pay his bill and that he was doing this while at the same time he was blocking the garage exit.

   (d) Officer Clark and I received a call involving a complaint from the attendant at the Metro Parking Garage. He stated that a man, who appeared to him to be drunk, was behaving in a belligerent manner. The attendant stated that the man refused to pay his bill and was presently blocking the garage exit.

9.   I saw two men leaving the club.
     One had red, spiked hair.
     One had a white tank top and baggy shorts on.
     Both men were running as they exited the club.

   (a) I saw two men leaving the club. Both men were running. One man had red, spiked hair. The other man had on a tank top and shorts.

   (b) I saw two men running out of the club. One of the men had red, spiked hair. The other was wearing a white tank top and baggy shorts.

   (c) Two men leaving the club running. The one man had red, spiked hair and the other one was wearing shorts that were of the baggy type and a tank top that was white in color.

   (d) I saw two men leaving from the club. One man had on a tank top. It was white. He also had on baggy shorts. The other man had red hair that was spiked. Both men were running.

GO ON TO THE NEXT PAGE.

10. **We investigated a complaint.**
    This was a new complaint.
    We questioned several witnesses.
    None of the witnesses was able to give us information relative to the complaint.

    (a) While investigating a complaint, we interviewed several witnesses. This was a new complaint and none of the witnesses told us anything we needed to know.

    (b) We investigated a complaint. It was a new one. We questioned several witnesses with no success.

    (c) While investigating a new complaint, we questioned several witnesses. The witnesses were unable to provide us with any information relative to the complaint.

    (d) Investigating a complaint, we interviewed several witnesses. The complaint was new and the witnesses could provide us with no relevant information regarding this complaint.

11. **I was assigned to investigate a complaint by the Whitesell construction site foreman.**
    The foreman complained that striking workers were blocking the entrance to the construction site.
    I drove to the site in my patrol vehicle without lights or siren.
    Three striking workers were present, but the entrance was not blocked.

    (a) Three striking workers were present at the Whitesell construction site I had been called to by the foreman. The entrance was not blocked.

    (b) I investigated a complaint by the Whitesell construction site foreman that the site's entrance was being blocked by striking workers. Upon arrival, I observed three striking workers, but the entrance to the site was not blocked.

    (c) Having been called to the construction site by the foreman of the construction project, he was complaining about a blocked construction entrance. I found the entrance open and three striking workers present at the time.

    (d) Three striking workers were present at the Whitesell construction entrance I had been called upon to investigate by the foreman.

GO ON TO THE NEXT PAGE.

12. **Officer Ventry and I were assigned to investigate a complaint of vandalism at the cemetery.**
   We drove to the cemetery.
   The gates were locked.

   (a) We investigated a complaint of vandalism but were unable to pursue the investigation because the gates were locked.

   (b) Officer Ventry and I drove to the cemetery to investigate a complaint of vandalism.

   (c) Officer Ventry and I, assigned to investigate a vandalism complaint at the cemetery, drove to the site and found the gates locked.

   (d) Our team was not able to investigate anything because the gates were locked at the scene of the cemetery where we were called.

GO ON TO THE NEXT PAGE.

13. Officers Drake and Salem called me to the front of the building.
There was a young couple standing there.
The young woman was carrying a newborn baby, who did not appear to be more than 30 days old.
The young woman was holding the baby while the young man stood near.
Drake and Salem said the couple wanted to leave the child at the police station.
Drake and Salem did not question the couple. Officer Drake took the child.
This was in accordance with the Safe Haven Infant Protection Act.

(a) Upon being called to the front of the station, I observed that Officers Drake and Salem abided by the Safe Haven Infant Protection Act, by not questioning a young married couple who were in the process of abandoning their infant at the front of the building.

(b) I was called to the front of the building, where Officers Drake and Salem advised me that a young man and woman wanted to leave an infant at the police station. The baby did not appear to be more than 30 days old. In accordance with the Safe Haven Infant Protection Act, Officer Drake took custody of the child and did not question the couple about the matter.

(c) At the front of our building, I was called by Officers Drake and Salem. Both officers related to me that there was a young couple who wanted to abandon their newborn baby at police headquarters and the baby was not more than the required thirty days old. Based on the Safe Haven Infant Protection Act, I advised the officers not to ask any questions of the couple.

(d) Officers Drake and Salem, while at the front of the station, called me to advise that they were taking custody of a 30-day-old baby who was just left by its parents in accordance with the Safe Haven Infant Protection Act.

GO ON TO THE NEXT PAGE.

14. I saw three girls leaving the train station.
One of the girls carried a pair blue sneakers.
Two of the girls wore school uniforms.
All three girls were running.

(a) I saw three girls running from the train station. Two wore school uniforms; one carried a pair of blue sneakers.

(b) Wearing school uniforms and blue sneakers, I saw three girls run from the train station.

(c) Running from the train station, I saw three girls. Two of the girls were wearing their school uniforms and one of them wore blue sneakers.

(d) Of the three girls I saw leaving the train station, two wore school uniforms, one carried her sneakers, and they were all running quickly.

15. I saw two men get out of a car.
One man wore a red baseball cap.
He wore it backward.
The other man was bald.
The car was a late model Ford Ltd.
It was black or dark blue.

(a) The car the two men got out of was a dark one. It might have been black or blue. It was a late model Ford Ltd. One man wore a red baseball cap backwards. One man was bald.

(b) I saw two men get out of a late model Ford Ltd. The car was dark, probably black or dark blue. One of the men wore a red baseball cap turned backwards. The other man was bald.

(c) Getting out of the dark Ford Ltd., I saw two men. One of the men was bald and the other wore a backwards red baseball cap.

(d) Two men got out of a car. The car was a late model Ford Ltd. The car was black or blue. There was a bald man and a man with a baseball cap. The man who had the baseball cap was not bald, but he was wearing the cap backwards.

END OF EXERCISE

1. (a) During questioning, the interviewee gave her name as Madonna. According to my partner, this was not the interviewee's real name.

2. (b) I observed four juveniles leaving the Wawa store. Three carried backpacks and one carried a large radio.

3. (b) Officer Collins and I, assigned to investigate a warehouse burglary, drove to the warehouse and found it closed and secure.

4. (c) My review of Officer Tompkins' preliminary investigation report revealed several report writing problems, such as 1 too many erasures; 2 not completing the "Who, What, Where, When, Why and How" of the incident, and 3 failing to sign the report. I recommend this officer receive refresher training in writing proper reports.

5. (d) During the investigation of a "loud music" call, the first such call from this address, we interviewed several angry neighbors.

6. (c) Officer Blue and I were called by a security official at Big Mart. Upon arrival at the store, we learned that a twelve-year-old boy was caught shoplifting. The boy had activated the store's alarm when he walked out with a Gameboy valued at $70.

7. (a) I was called to 119 East 14th Street by a woman whose pocketbook was taken from her home. She stated that she had left the front door unlocked while she was in the backyard gardening.

8. (d) Officer Clark and I received a call involving a complaint from the attendant at the Metro Parking Garage. He stated that a man, who appeared to him to be drunk, was behaving in a belligerent manner. The attendant stated that the man refused to pay his bill and was presently blocking the garage exit.

9. (b) I saw two men running out of the club. One of the men had red, spiked hair. The other was wearing a white tank top and baggy shorts.

10. (c) While investigating a new complaint, we questioned several witnesses. The witnesses were unable to provide us with any information relative to the complaint.

11. (b) I investigated a complaint by the Whitesell construction site foreman that the site's entrance was being blocked by striking workers. Upon arrival, I observed three striking workers, but the entrance to the site was not blocked.

12. (c) Officer Ventry and I, assigned to investigate a vandalism complaint at the cemetery, drove to the site and found the gates locked.

13. (b) I was called to the front of the building, where Officers Drake and Salem advised me that a young man and woman wanted to leave an infant at the police station. The baby did not appear to be more than 30 days old. In accordance with the Safe Haven Infant Protection Act, Officer Drake took custody of the child and did not question the couple about the matter.

14. (a) I saw three girls running from the train station. Two wore school uniforms; one carried a pair of blue sneakers.

15. (b) I saw two men get out of a late model Ford Ltd. The car was dark, probably black or dark blue. One of the men wore a red baseball cap turned backwards. The other man was bald.

The proper use of the English language is a must for Effective Law Enforcement Reporting. Reports should not only be capable being understood, they should also be incapable of being misunderstood.

Directions:
Items #1 – #25 consist of a series of excerpts from recently taken field notes. Review the field notes presented and select the statement — (a), (b), (c), or (d) — which BEST reports what occurred at the time the field notes were written.

GO ON TO THE NEXT PAGE.

1. three subjects exited doorway
   two wearing black raincoats
   one carrying blue umbrella
   drove away quickly in a blue/GMC
   unable to make out license plate

   (a) Observed three subjects exit the doorway of the building of which two were wearing black raincoats while the third was carrying a blue umbrella. The subjects entered a blue GMC with unknown license number and drove off quickly.

   (b) Three subjects exited the building quickly and entered a blue GMC that departed the area at a high rate of speed. The license number was not recorded and the three subjects had two black raincoats and a blue umbrella.

   (c) While answering a robbery call, I observed subject run out of the building carrying blue umbrellas while two of the subjects were wearing black coats. The subjects jumped into a blue GMC and sped away without exposing the truck's license plate number.

   (d) I observed three subjects exit the doorway of the building. Two of the subjects were wearing black raincoats and one of the three was carrying a blue umbrella. The subjects entered a blue GMC and drove off quickly. I was unable to determine the vehicle's license number.

GO ON TO THE NEXT PAGE.

2. **assigned aggravated assault investigation**
responded to factory picket line
requested to speak with witnesses
witnesses refused to speak
partner/I unable to further investigation

(a) Upon responding to the factory to speak with potential witnesses, we met with resistance as the witnesses refused to speak with us which resulted in our not being able to further the investigation.

(b) My partner and I responded to the local factory where the picketers became agitated at our presence forcing us to abandon the investigation.

(c) My partner and I responded to the factory picket line in reference to an aggravated assault investigation. Upon arrival, we attempted to speak with witnesses, but they would not cooperate with us. This stalled any further investigation at this point in time.

(d) Upon being assigned the aggravated assault follow-up investigation, I soon learned that the witnesses were not willing to speak with the police and my partner and I closed the investigation out due to the uncooperative witnesses.

GO ON TO THE NEXT PAGE.

3. **9th and Horner Streets**
   male standing on corner talking to female
   female gave male money
   male gave female small brown package
   both subjects were investigatively detained
   consent search revealed contraband

   (a) I observed a female subject approach a male subject on the corner of 9th and Horner Street where the female subject passed money to the male in return for a brown package. Both subjects were investigatively detained and a consent search revealed the contraband.

   (b) An unknown male passed a brown package to an unknown male for an undetermined sum of money causing us to arrest them and find contraband as a result of a subsequent search of their possessions.

   (c) After observing a male talking to a female on the corner of 9th and Horner Street, I observed the female hand the male money followed by the male handing the female a small brown package. I detained the female and found the contraband after receiving her consent to search.

   (d) Male subjects stood on the corner of 9th and Horner Street where females approached and passed the males a package which led to an investigative detention and later arrest.

GO ON TO THE NEXT PAGE.

4. juvenile male at corner
female standing near door
adult male pointing gun at cashier
juvenile male fled east
other two fled west on foot

(a) Upon arrival, a juvenile male was standing on the street corner while an adult male held a gun to the cashier. The adult male fled east while the juvenile male fled west with a female.

(b) Upon arrival, an adult male was holding a gun to the cashier as an adult female was standing near the door and another juvenile male stood on the street corner. The adult male and female fled west while the juvenile fled east on foot.

(c) Upon arrival, three unknown subjects robbed the store and escaped the capture by fleeing on foot.

(d) Upon my arrival, a juvenile male was standing on the corner, a female was standing near the door of the store, and an adult male was pointing a gun at the cashier. The adult male and the female fled west on foot while the male juvenile fled east.

GO ON TO THE NEXT PAGE.

5. **Witness #1 statement:**
   blue Chevy traveling east on Western Blvd.
   red Ford traveling north on South St.
   red Ford had green light
   blue Chevy did not stop
   front of Ford struck side of Chevy

(a) Witness reported observing an accident at the intersection of Western Blvd. and South Street which involved a blue Chevy running a red light and striking the side of a red Ford causing injuries to the occupants of both vehicles.

(b) Witness #1 observed the red Ford traveling north on South Street entering the intersection of Western Blvd. when the blue Chevy ran the red light and struck the passenger side of the red Ford.

(c) Witness #1 reported observing a red Ford traveling north on South Street through the green light into the intersection of Western Blvd., when a blue Chevy, which was traveling east on Western Blvd., failed to stop and entered the intersection, resulting in the front of the red Ford striking the side of the blue Chevy.

(d) Witness #1 reported observing a red Ford traveling north on South Street through the green light into the intersection of Western Blvd. when a blue Chevy, which was traveling east on Western Blvd., failed to stop and entered the intersection, resulting in the front of the blue Chevy striking the side of the red Ford.

GO ON TO THE NEXT PAGE.

6. missing 9-year-old-girl
    crying and asking mother to watch mall muppet show
    last seen near mall water fountain
    has walked off in the past
    previously found wandering near area

    (a) A 9-year-old child was crying after wandering in the area near a mall water fountain because she went to watch a muppet show. The mother has misplaced her daughter in the past.

    (b) A mother reported that her 9-year-old girl was missing in the mall. The child was last seen near the water fountain and was upset after not being allowed to watch the mall muppet show. The mother reported that the child had been missing in the past and is usually found wandering in the area.

    (c) Mother reported her 9-year-old daughter previously missing from near the mall water fountain. Mother reported finding the girl wandering in the area similar to other times that she has been missing. The girl was reportedly still upset because she missed the mall muppet show.

    (d) A child was reported missing at the local mall. The 9-year-old child was observed crying about wanting to watch a mall muppet show prior to wandering away from the area of the water fountain. The child's mother reported that he has been missing in the past.

GO ON TO THE NEXT PAGE.

7. woman jogging in park
   observed Caucasian male behind retaining wall as she passed
   black male emerged from wooded path
   woman struck from behind
   struck with hammer, unconscious
   medical test revealed sexual assault

(a) A woman was jogging in the park and observed a black male who was hiding behind the retaining wall when she ran past. The male later emerged from a wooded pathway and struck her with what she believed was a hammer. The hospital later determined that she had been sexually assaulted.

(b) A brutal attack and sexual assault occurred as a woman was jogging in the park. A Caucasian male emerged from behind a retaining wall and struck the woman with a hammer which enabled him and a black male to sexually assault her in a wooded pathway. The hospital medical records indicate that a sexual assault did in fact occur.

(c) A woman was jogging in the State Park when she was attacked by an unknown male and possibly sexually assaulted. The woman reported that prior to the assault she observed an unknown male hiding behind a retaining wall in the park and was subsequently attacked by an unknown male while jogging down a wooded pathway.

(d) A woman was jogging in the county park, when she observed a suspicious Caucasian male who appeared to be hiding behind a retaining wall. Shortly thereafter, she was attacked from behind by a black male who emerged from a wooded pathway and struck her in the head with a hammer, rendering her unconscious. The hospital medical records indicate that a sexual assault occurred.

GO ON TO THE NEXT PAGE.

8. doctor's office rear window broken in
   alarm physically disabled
   prescription pad and medications missing
   front door found ajar and unlocked by doctor

   (a) The doctor reported finding the door of his office unlocked and open and discovered that the window was smashed inward. The doctor reported that prescription medication and a prescription pad were missing and that the alarm had been disabled by the burglar.

   (b) The doctor reported finding the front door of his office unlocked and open and discovered that the rear window was smashed inward. The doctor reported that prescription medications were missing from the office. The alarm must have been physically disabled by the burglar as it did not sound.

   (c) A doctor's office was victimized by a burglar who successfully disabled the office alarm and stole prescription medications and prescription pads. The burglar entered through the broken rear window and exited through the front door after unlocking it.

   (d) The doctor reported finding the front door of his office unlocked and open and discovered that the rear window was broken inward. The doctor reported that prescription medication and a prescription pad were missing and that the alarm had been disabled by the burglar.

GO ON TO THE NEXT PAGE.

9. **Mail carrier on foot delivery**
   one brown pit bull w/red collar in fenced area
   one white pit bull w/blue collar in front window
   mail carrier attacked by black pit bull
   black pit bull wearing red tag on blue collar
   dog fled area after attack

   (a) The mail carrier was delivering mail on foot when attacked by a black pit bull wearing a blue tag and a red collar. The black pit bull ran from the area after the attack. Prior to the attack, the mail carrier recalled seeing a brown pit bull with a red collar in a fenced-in area and a white pit bull with a blue collar in the front window of the house.

   (b) The mail carrier was delivering mail on foot when attacked by a black pit bull wearing a red tag and a blue collar. The black pit bull ran from the area after the attack. Prior to the attack, the mail carrier recalled seeing a brown pit bull with a red collar in a fenced area and a white pit bull with a blue collar in the front window of the house.

   (c) The mail carrier was delivering mail on foot when attacked by a black pit bull wearing a red tag and a blue collar. The black pit bull ran from the area after the attack. Prior to the attack, the mail carrier recalled seeing a brown pit bull with a red collar in the front window of the house and a white pit bull with a blue collar in a fenced area.

   (d) A mail carrier was delivering mail when attacked by a pit bull. The carrier reported observing two other pit bulls in the yard and house prior to the attack. The carrier was bit on the leg and arm and required assistance in breaking free from the vicious dog.

GO ON TO THE NEXT PAGE.

10. store detective reports:
white male in aisle #2
two teen Asian females in aisle #3
one Asian female holding paper bag
white male placed meat in bag in aisle #3
Asian female and white male created diversion
other female walked out with merchandise

(a) A white male observed two Asian females standing in aisle #3 while another male was walking toward aisle #3 to place a stolen package of meat into a bag for one of the Asian females to carry out of the store. Upon a store detective approaching the Asian female, the male dropped a jar to create a diversion.

(b) A store detective noticed a white female and an Asian female creating a diversion by dropping a glass jar in aisle #2. The store detective then realized that the male subject had facilitated the shoplifting of a package of meat by placing the package of meat in a paper bag being held by an Asian female.

(c) The store detective observed a white male take a package of meat from aisle #2 to aisle #3 and place it in a paper bag being carried by a teen-age Asian female. The male and a second Asian female standing in aisle #3 created a diversion while the other female walked out of the store with the merchandise.

(d) A male observed two Asian females standing in aisle #3 while another male was walking toward aisle #3 from aisle #2 to place a stolen package of meat into a bag for one of the Asian females to carry out of the store. Upon a store detective approaching the Asian female, the male dropped a jar to create a diversion which allowed the two Asian females to leave the store safely.

GO ON TO THE NEXT PAGE.

11. **Took missing persons report**
    Person missing for five weeks
    Had been missing like this several times before

    (a) I took a report of a person missing for five weeks. The person had been missing like this several other times.

    (b) I took a report of a missing person missing for 5 weeks, but this was not the first time.

    (c) Even though the person had been missing like this before, I took a missing persons report. The person had been missing for 5 weeks.

    (d) I took a missing persons report of a person missing for five weeks. This same person had been missing before. The person had been missing for a similar amount of time.

12. **woman sitting at bar alone**
    bartender served a draft beer
    male subject approached woman
    woman briefly spoke with male
    next recollection was waking partly dressed
    found in alley next to bar

    (a) A woman reported that she suspected that she was drugged and sexually assaulted. She stated that she was sitting at the bar drinking a draft beer when a male subject approached her and engaged her in conversation. She was found in the alley partly dressed and could only recall the male approaching her in the bar, and then waking up and being partly dressed.

    (b) The woman reported that she suspected that she was drugged and sexually assaulted. She stated that she was sitting at the bar drinking a draft beer when a male subject approached her and engaged her in conversation. She next recalled waking partly dressed on the front sidewalk outside the closed bar.

    (c) The bartender reported serving a woman a draft beer and then observing a man approach and place an unknown substance in her glass. The bartender stated that the woman left with the male and later returned to the bar stating that she was sexually assaulted in the alley next to the bar.

    (d) The bartender reported that in the evening he recalled serving a woman a beer. He then observed a heavy set man approach and place what he believed was a narcotic substance in her glass. The bartender stated that the woman then immediately left with the male and later was found outside the bar partly dressed.

GO ON TO THE NEXT PAGE.

13. home invasion of residence
victim owner of Chinese restaurant terrorized
five Asian male gang members; seven Asian victims tied up
used hand-held automatic weapons; $10,000 cash stolen

(a) Asian male gang members forcibly invaded the home of a Chinese family by utilizing hand-held automatic weapons. During the incident, seven occupants of the home were tied up and terrorized while $10,000 in cash was stolen.

(b) Five Asian male gang members forcibly invaded the home of a Chinese restaurant owner by utilizing hand-held automatic weapons. During the incident, seven occupants of the home were tied up and terrorized while $10,000 in cash was stolen.

(c) Five Asian males broke into the home of a Chinese food restaurant owner by utilizing physical force. While terrorizing the seven occupants of the home, the five males stole $10,000 in cash and physically assaulted the five members of the household.

(d) Asian male gang members forcibly invaded the home of a Chinese family by utilizing hand-held automatic weapons. While terrorizing the five occupants of the home, the males stole $10,000 in cash and physically assaulted the three members of the household.

GO ON TO THE NEXT PAGE.

14. white male with trench coat entered store
    walked to rear of store
    approached from behind cashier
    produced sawed-off shotgun
    received $84.00 cash
    fled east on foot

(a) The clerk reported that the male suspect entered the door and approached her from behind. The subject produced a sawed-off shotgun and was given $84.00 prior to fleeing the store on foot.

(b) A white male subject entered the back of the store and approached the clerk from behind. The subject was wearing a trench coat and was holding a sawed-off shotgun. The clerk gave the subject $84.00 from the cash register and the subject fled east on foot.

(c) The clerk reported that the white male suspect entered the front door, walked toward the rear of the store, and then approached her from behind. The subject produced a sawed-off shotgun from beneath his trench coat and was given $84.00 prior to fleeing east from the store on foot.

(d) A white male subject entered the store and walked to the rear of the store. The subject was wearing a trench coat and was holding a sawed-off shotgun. The clerk gave the subject $84.00 from the cash register and the subject fled on foot.

GO ON TO THE NEXT PAGE.

15. female bleeding from mouth
husband's right hand bleeding
dishes broken on floor
male hostile toward officers
male resisted arrest

(a) A female was found bleeding from her mouth after her husband struck her with his right fist. The dishes were broken on the floor. The husband was arrested after becoming hostile toward the officers.

(b) A female was found bleeding from her mouth after her husband struck her with his right fist. I also noticed broken dishes on the floor. The male subject was hostile toward the officers and resisted their attempt to place him under arrest.

(c) The female complainant reported that she was bleeding from her mouth and pointed out dishes broken on the floor. Her husband's left hand was bleeding. The male subject exhibited hostility at the presence police officers and resisted his arrest for the domestic assault.

(d) A male subject resisted arrest after officers responded to his residence with a report of a domestic assault. His wife reported that she tried to defend herself by breaking dishes but he punched her in the stomach causing her to lose her breath temporarily. She stated that she exited the residence and asked her neighbor to call the police. Officers arrested the husband for the assault.

GO ON TO THE NEXT PAGE.

16. three males observed behind school
two wearing ski masks
one wearing grey jacket
two subjects fled west into woods
one subject fled north across roadway

(a) The witness reported observing three male subjects hiding behind the school while the school was closed. Upon seeing the witness, two of the subjects fled west while the third fled north. Two subjects were wearing ski masks while the third subject was wearing a grey jacket.

(b) A witness reported observing three male subjects hiding behind the school. Upon seeing the witness, two of the subjects fled west into the woods while the third fled north across the roadway. The third subject was wearing a grey jacket while the first two were wearing ski masks.

(c) A witness observed male subjects hiding behind the school. The witness reported observing two of the subjects flee north into the woods while the third fled west across the roadway. One subject was wearing a grey jacket while the other two were wearing ski masks.

(d) A witness observed three male subjects behind the closed school. Two of the subjects were wearing ski masks while one of the three was wearing a grey jacket. Two of the subjects fled into the wooded area on the west side of the school while the other subject fled north across the roadway.

GO ON TO THE NEXT PAGE.

17. took "missing persons" report
    father reports 47-year-old son missing
    missing for three weeks
    has been missing before but not for this long
    son has drug problems

    (a) I took a "missing persons" report from a very distraught father. He stated that his son had been missing for 3 weeks. He said that he had a history of drug abuse. The son had gone away before, but never for such a long period of time. The father was worried that his son was dead somewhere.

    (b) I took a "missing persons" report from a father who said that he had not heard from his 47-year-old son in 3 weeks. He stated that his son did have a history of drug abuse and had been missing for short periods of time before this incident.

    (c) A father submitted a "missing persons" report about his 47-year-old son who was a drug abuser. The son had sometimes been missing before, but he had never been missing for so long before.

    (d) After his 47-year-old son had been missing for three weeks, a father came in to fill out a "missing persons" report. Because of drug abuse, the son had been missing before but not for so long. This was the longest he had ever been missing.

18. asked suspect for her full name; replied, "Kitty Katt"
    partner familiar with suspect
    he says "Kitty Katt" is often used by suspect as an alias

    (a) I asked the suspect her name and she said it was "Kitty Katt." My partner directed to me this was an alias used by the suspect.

    (b) Kitty Katt gave me an alias name while I was questioning her. This was supported by my partner who was very familiar with the suspect.

    (c) During questioning, the suspect gave her name as Kitty Katt. According to my partner this was not the suspect's real name, but an alias frequently used by her.

    (d) When we questioned the suspect, she provided us with her name as Kitty Katt. According to my partner, this name was an alias.

GO ON TO THE NEXT PAGE.

19. I interviewed a suspect picked up for shoplifting
    Said name was Peter Paul
    Said he didn't mean to leave without paying for bracelet

    (a) Peter Paul, the shoplifting suspect I interviewed, said he did not intentionally leave the store without paying for the bracelet.

    (b) Accused of shoplifting a bracelet, Peter Paul said he did not mean to shoplift.

    (c) After shoplifting a bracelet, Peter Paul said he did not mean it.

    (d) Interviewing Peter Paul, a suspect suspected of shoplifting, provided me with the information that he did not mean to take the bracelet without paying for it.

20. assigned with partner to a job to investigate
    job—female child missing from mall; drove to mall
    Found child with mother

    (a) My partner and I were called to find a missing child. After we drove there we found out the child was found. The child and mother were together.

    (b) We got a call about a female child who was missing from the mall. When we got there we found out the child was not missing anymore.

    (c) Office Smith and I investigated a call about a female child missing from the mall. We drove to the mall and, upon our arrival, learned that the child had been found and was with her mother.

    (d) Officer Smith, my partner, and I were assigned to investigate a call about a female child missing from the mall. We drove to the mall. We found out the child had already been found. We found the child with her mother.

GO ON TO THE NEXT PAGE.

21. two young men observed behind drugstore
one wearing dark ski mask
one wearing grey windbreaker
both subjects ran east down alley
one ran straight across roadway
one turned right on 9th St.

(a) Two witnesses reported seeing two young men hanging out behind the drugstore. When the young men noticed the witnesses, they ran up the alley. The witnesses noted that one young man wore a dark ski cap and one wore a light jacket.

(b) Witnesses noticed two young men behind the drugstore. One young man was wearing a grey ski mask and the other was wearing a grey windbreaker. When the boys became aware of the witnesses the boys ran down the alley where one ran straight ahead and one ran to the right of 9th St.

(c) Witnesses observed two young men behind the drugstore. One subject was wearing a dark ski mask and the other was wearing a grey windbreaker. Both subjects ran east down the alley to 9th St. One ran straight across 9th St. while the other ran to the right down 9th St.

(d) Two young boys were witnessed behind the drugstore. One was wearing a dark ski mask and one was wearing a grey jacket. The boys fled west down the alley. They ran to 9th St., where they separated and one went across the street and one went right down the street.

GO ON TO THE NEXT PAGE.

22. assigned aggravated assault investigation
responded to address given
asked to speak to complainant
complainant refused to speak
unable to investigate further

(a) I responded to an aggravated assault complaint. The complainant refused to speak with me, which, at that moment, prevented further investigation.

(b) Upon responding to an aggravated assault complaint, I tried to meet with the complainant, who refused to see me, so I ended the investigation.

(c) When I was assigned the aggravated assault investigation, I went to the address given. When I got there, the complainant refused to speak to me so, the investigation ended.

(d) I was not able to complete this investigation of an aggravated assault because the complainant would not speak to me.

23. missing four-year-old boy
crying because he wanted to go to the pet store
last seen in Sears' appliance department
mother reports has gone off on own before
has always been found quickly

(a) A four-year-old child was reported missing from the local shopping center. The child had wanted to go to the pet store, but her mother took the child to the appliance department at Sears. The mother stated the child has wandered off at other times but has always been found quickly.

(b) A mother reported her previously missing four-year-old boy missing again. This time he was upset because she wouldn't take him from Sears to the pet store. He is usually found quickly.

(c) A mother reported her four-year-old boy missing from Sears. The boy was last seen in the appliance department and was crying because he wanted to go to the pet store. The mother reported that the boy has wandered off before, but has always been found quickly.

(d) A mother who had previously lost her child before, reported him missing from Sears' appliance department. The four-year-old had wanted to go to the pet store. When he has been missing before he has always been found in a speedy and competent manner.

GO ON TO THE NEXT PAGE.

24. observe three teens around UPS truck (stopped)
driver in local coffee shop making quick delivery
driver returns to truck, sees three deliveries missing from truck
one teen had blue tank top
one was barefoot
two wore Mets caps

(a) A UPS driver called to report several packages missing from his delivery truck. He said he left his truck to make a local delivery. Witnesses reported seeing three teens around the empty truck. One of the teens was not wearing shoes and was wearing a blue tank top. The other two teens were wearing Mets baseball caps. The delivery the driver was making was at the coffee shop.

(b) Three teens were observed by witnesses hanging around a UPS truck that had a missing driver and was missing several packages. The driver was in the coffee shop. One of the teens was described as being barefoot. One was wearing a blue tank top. Some wore Mets caps.

(c) A barefoot teen, a teen in blue tank top, and two teens wearing Mets caps were seen hanging around a UPS truck that reported several packages missing. The truck's driver was in a coffee shop. He was making a delivery.

(d) A UPS driver reported several packages missing from his truck after he returned from making a quick delivery at the local coffee shop. Witnesses reported seeing three teenagers hanging around the empty truck. One teen wore a blue tank top. One was barefoot. Two of the teens wore Mets baseball caps.

GO ON TO THE NEXT PAGE.

25. pharmacist reports burglary
pharmacy's alarm purposely disabled
rear window broken
all bags containing filled prescriptions were missing
front door found unlocked by pharmacist

(a) A pharmacist reported that the alarm to the pharmacy was not working. He said that when he arrived the back door was unlocked. He found all the bags containing filled prescriptions were missing. He also reported a front window broken.

(b) A pharmacist reported that all the bags containing filled prescriptions were missing from the pharmacy. When he arrived in the morning to open, he found the front door unlocked and the alarm disabled. A rear window had also been broken.

(c) A pharmacist reported finding the door of the pharmacy unlocked, the window broken, and the alarm not functioning. Missing from shelves were bags of already filled prescriptions.

(d) A pharmacist called to report a burglary at his pharmacy. He reported that when he went to work in the morning he noticed the front door was unlocked. He noticed that the burglar had disabled the alarm, entered through the rear window, which was broken, and had stolen all of the bags of already filled prescriptions. He reported some of the bags contained medication that could be sold illegally on the street.

END OF EXERCISE

Remember, field notes are designed to
refresh recollection.

1. (d) I observed three subjects exit the doorway of the building. Two of the subjects were wearing black raincoats and one of the three was carrying a blue umbrella. The subjects entered a blue GMC and drove off quickly. I was unable to determine the vehicle's license number. *The other answer choices contain information not set forth in the field notes.*

2. (c) My partner and I responded to the factory picket line in reference to an aggravated assault investigation. Upon arrival, we attempted to speak with witnesses, but they would not cooperate with us. This stalled any further investigation at this point in time. *Choices* (a) *and* (b) *are missing the "aggravated assault investigation." Choice* (b)*'s use of the words "agitated" and "abandon" is not reflected in the field notes. Choice* (d) *contains information not contained in the field notes.*

3. (c) After observing a male talking to a female on the corner of 9th and Horner Streets, I observed the female hand the male money followed by the male handing the female a small brown package. I detained the female and found the contraband after receiving her consent to search. *Choices* (a) *and* (d) *contain detail not set forth in the field notes. Choice* (b) *contains an error regarding who received the package.*

4. (d) Upon arrival, a juvenile male was standing on the corner, a female was standing near the door of the store, and an adult male was pointing a gun at the cashier. The adult male and the female fled west on foot while the male juvenile fled east. *Choice (a) contains error in directions. Choice (b) describes female as an adult (not in field notes). Choice (c) is missing too many facts.*

5. (c) Witness #1 reported observing a red Ford traveling north on South Street through the green light into the intersection of Western Blvd., when a blue Chevy, which was traveling east on Western Blvd., failed to stop and entered the intersection, resulting in the front of the red Ford striking the side of the blue Chevy. *Choice (a) is a poorly-worded, run-on sentence. Choice (b) contains information not reflected in the field notes. Choice (d) inaccurately describes the color of the Chevy and the color of the For(d)*

6. (b) A mother reported that her 9-year-old girl was missing in the mall. The child was last seen near the water fountain and was upset after not being allowed to watch the mall muppet show. The mother reported that the child had been missing in the past and is usually found wandering in the area. *Choice (a) contains information not found in the field notes. Choice (c) also contains information not found in the notes, along with inaccurate language, "previously missing." Choice (d) has a poor choice of words in the phrase, "crying about wanting," and uses the word "he" to describe the missing 9-year-old girl.*

7. (d) A woman was jogging in the county park, when she observed a suspicious Caucasian male who appeared to be hiding behind a retaining wall. Shortly thereafter, she was attacked from behind by a black male who emerged from a wooded pathway and struck her in the head with a hammer, rendering her unconscious. The hospital medical records indicate that a sexual assault occurred. *Choices (a), (b) and (c) all contain facts not reflected in the field notes.*

8. (d) The doctor reported finding the front door of his office unlocked and open and discovered that the rear window was broken inward. The doctor reported that prescription medication and a prescription pad were missing and that the alarm had been disabled by the burglar. The use of the word "smashed" in choices (a) and (b) changes the perspective of the event. *Choice (a) fails to report that the "front" door was found ajar, and both (a) and (b) have facts not reflected in the notes. In addition, choice (b) fails to report the missing prescription pa(d) In choice (c), "office was victimized" is a poor choice of words. Also, the field notes do not indicate that a burglar "successfully disabled" anything. Use of the word "pads" inaccurately reports that more than one prescription pad was taken.*

9. (b) The mail carrier was delivering mail on foot when attacked by a black pit bull wearing a red tag and a blue collar. The black pit bull ran from the area after the attack. Prior to the attack, the mail carrier recalled seeing a brown pit bull with a red collar in a fenced area and a white pit bull with a blue collar in the front window of the house. *Choice (a) incorrectly reports the color of the tag and collar. Choices (c) and (d) contain details not reflected in the field notes.*

10. (c) The store detective observed a white male take a package of meat from aisle #2 to aisle #3 and place it in a paper bag being carried by a teen-age Asian female. The male and a second Asian female standing in aisle #3 dropped a glass jar on the floor while the other female walked out of the store with the merchandise. *Choices (a) and (b) contain facts not set forth in the field notes. Choice (d) inaccurately reports who dropped the jar to create a diversion and who left the store safely.*

11. (a) I took a report of a person missing for five weeks. The person had been missing like this several other times. *Choice (b)'s use of the phrase, "but this was not the first time," is too confusing. Is this the first time the person was missing or the first time such a report was taken? Choice (c). has a spelling error (thought) and is also confusing. Choice (d) is poorly written and is unclear in the use of the phrase, "missing for a similar amount of time."*

12. (a) A woman reported that she suspected that she was drugged and sexually assaulted. She stated that she was sitting at the bar drinking a draft beer when a male subject approached her and engaged her in conversation. She was found in the alley partly dressed and could only recall the male approaching her in the bar, and then waking up and being partly dressed. *Choices (b), (c) and (d) all contain errors regarding where the woman was foun(d) Choice (d) contains facts not set forth in the field notes.*

13. (b) Five Asian male gang members forcibly invaded the home of a Chinese restaurant owner by utilizing hand-held automatic weapons. During the incident, seven occupants of the home were tied up and terrorized while $10,000 in cash was stolen. *Choice (a) is missing facts. Choices (c) and (d) contain inaccurate facts.*

14. (c) The clerk reported that the white male suspect entered the front door, walked toward the rear of the store, and then approached her from behind. The subject produced a sawed-off shotgun from beneath his trench coat and was given $84.00 prior to fleeing east from the store on foot. *Choice (a) adds that the suspect "entered the door," instead of "store," and is missing the fact relating to the "trench coat." Choice (b) incorrectly reports that the suspect entered "the back" of the store. Choice (d) is missing several facts.*

15. (b) A female was found bleeding from her mouth after her husband struck her with his right fist. I also noticed broken dishes on the floor. The male subject was hostile toward the officers and resisted their attempt to place him under arrest. *Choice (a) is missing the facts of the husband's bleeding right hand and the male's resisting arrest. Choice (c) incorrectly reports that the female complainant "pointed out" dishes, and that the husband's "left" hand was bleeding. Choice (d) contains detail not found in the field notes.*

16. (d) A witness observed three male subjects behind the closed school. Two of the subjects were wearing ski masks while one of the three was wearing a grey jacket. Two of the subjects fled into the wooded area on the west side of the school while the other subject fled north across the roadway. *Choice (a) contains facts not found in the field notes, and is missing the fact that two subjects fled west "into the woods." The use of the phrase, the "third" subject, in choices (a) and (b) presents a distinction not drawn by the field notes. Choice (c) has several errors in the subjects' direction of flight, as well as an improper distinction drawn by the use of "the other two were wearing...."*

17. (b) I took a "missing persons" report from a father, who said that he had not heard from his 47-year-old son in 3 weeks. He stated that his son did have a history of drug abuse and had been missing for short periods of time before this incident. *Choice (a) contains information not found in the field notes. Choice (c) contains an inaccurate statement regarding the "missing persons" report, and the second sentence is poorly written. The second sentence of choice (d) is not accurate.*

18. (c) During my questioning, the suspect gave her name as Kitty Katt. According to my partner this was not the suspect's real name, but an alias frequently used by her. *Choices (a) and (b) are poorly written. Choice (d) incorrectly suggests that two persons were doing the questioning.*

19. (a) Peter Paul, the shoplifting suspect I interviewed, said he did not intentionally leave the store without paying for the bracelet. *Choice (b) fails to use an "active" writing style and is not entirely accurate. Choice (c) is missing facts, and choice (d) is missing a subject for the "provided me" clause.*

20. (c) Office Smith and I investigated a call about a female child missing from the mall. We drove to the mall and, upon our arrival, learned that the child had been found and was with her mother. *Choice (a) contains inaccurate facts, and choices (b) and (d) are very poorly worde(d)*

21. (c) Witnesses observed two young men behind the drugstore. One subject was wearing a dark ski mask and the other was wearing a grey windbreaker. Both subjects ran east down the alley to 9th St. One ran straight across 9th St. while the other ran to the right down 9th St. *Choice (a) uses an unclear pronoun, "they," and incorrectly reports that one man wore a dark ski "cap." Choice (b) incorrectly describes the ski mask as "grey." Choice (d) incorrectly reports that two young "boys" were "witnessed," and contains an error in the direction of flight.*

22. (a) I responded to an aggravated assault complaint. The complainant refused to speak with me, which, at that moment, prevented further investigation. *Choices (b) and (c) both incorrectly report that the investigation was "ende(d)" Choice (d) is not correct for there is a substantive difference between being unable "to complete this investigation," and, as set forth in the field notes, "unable to investigate further."*

23. (c) A mother reported her four-year-old boy missing from Sears. The boy was last seen in the appliance department and was crying because he wanted to go to the pet store. The mother reported that the boy has wandered off before, but has always been found quickly. *Choice (a) omits the child's gender, and choices (b) and (d) are poorly written.*

24. (d) A UPS driver reported several packages missing from his truck after he returned from making a quick delivery at the local coffee shop. Witnesses reported seeing three teenagers hanging around the empty truck. One teen wore a blue tank top. One was barefoot. Two of the teens wore Mets baseball caps. *Choices (a), (b) and (c) contain inaccurate facts. Note also that choice (c) implies that there are four teens instead of three.*

25. (b) A pharmacist reported that all the bags containing filled prescriptions were missing from the pharmacy. When he arrived in the morning to open, he found the front door unlocked and the alarm disabled. A rear window had also been broken. *Choice (a) contains inaccurate facts and choice (c) is missing facts. Choice (d)'s conclusion that the burglar disabled the alarm is not set forth in the field notes. In addition, the last sentence of choice (d) adds a fact not set forth in the notes.*

A common error in English grammar and usage relates to "subject-verb agreement." Subjects and verbs must be brought into line—they must agree. This means that a singular subject must be matched with a singular verb and a plural subject must be matched with a plural verb. Most mistakes in agreement involve the misidentification of the precise subject or number of subject(s) or the losing sight of what words go together. To avoid errors in subject-verb agreement, you must know how to pick out the subject for every verb you use and how to tell whether that subject is singular or plural.

Another area of error relates to pronoun agreement. Personal pronouns have distinctive singular and plural forms, for example, *he/they, his/their, him/them,* etc. To determine whether to use a singular or plural pronoun, reference must be made to its antecedent (the word, phrase, or clause to which it refers), and pronouns must agree in form (singular or plural) with their antecedents. Most of the rules that apply to the agreement of subjects and verbs apply to the agreement of pronouns and their antecedents.

Directions:
Circle the correct verb or pronoun.

1. My gun and baton [is] [are] on my belt.

2. Enclosed [is] [are] my application and a check for the fee.

3. Also on my list of all-time great leaders [is] [are] Martin Luther King, Jr.

4. More rewarding than the salary [is] [are] the public approval, the subordinate approval and the opportunity to influence the careers of others.

5. How important to you [is] [are] your gun and badge?

GO ON TO THE NEXT PAGE.

6. [Has] [Have] the Domestic Violence Policy and the Drug Screening Policy begun to affect employee morale?

7. [Do] [Does] a correction officer and a police officer have a lot in common?

8. There [is] [are] a police officer at the front door and two reporters at the back.

9. Everybody on the 4-12 shift has satisfied [their] [his] in-service training requirement.

10. In those days there [was] [were] only 35 officers on the Department and two dispatchers.

11. The sum and substance of the class [was] [were] "proper preparation."

12. The long and short of it [is] [are] that you must study to do well.

13. A friend and colleague of mine [is] [are] in charge of the Detective Bureau.

14. My sergeant, as well as my lieutenant, [expect] [expects] that it will be done by the end of the day.

15. Tom, as well as Sam, [prefer] [prefers] coffee to tea.

16. The strength of the platoon, along with the high morale, [have] [has] made working here very pleasant.

17. None of the officers completed [their] [his] assignment.

18. Officer Robinson is the only one of the five day shift officers who [has] [have] entered the weight lifting competition who [is] [are] likely to win.

19. Either the captain or the lieutenant [is] [are] responsible for the completion of the crime statistics.

20. The number of articles about sexual scandal in government written by members of the media during the Clinton administration [seem] [seems] to grow larger every month.

END OF EXERCISE

1. My gun and baton **are** on my belt. A subject consisting of two or more words joined by *and* is, in most cases, a compound subject requiring a plural verb. Here, the subject, *gun and baton*, is compound and therefore requires a plural verb.

2. Enclosed **are** my application and a check for the fee. Here, the subject, *application and a check*, is inverted, with the verb appearing before the subject. The subject is compound and requires a plural verb.

3. Also on my list of all-time great leaders **is** Martin Luther King, Jr. The subject, *Martin Luther King, Jr.*, is singular.

4. More rewarding than the salary **are** the public approval, the subordinate approval and the opportunity to influence the careers of others. Here, again, the plural subject is inverted.

5. How important to you **are** your gun and badge? The subject, *gun and badge*, is plural.

6. **Have** the Domestic Violence Policy and the Drug Screening Policy begun to affect employee morale? The subject, *Domestic Violence Policy and the Drug Screening Policy*, is compound, requiring a plural *have*.

7. **Do** a correction officer and a police officer have a lot in common? Change the question to a statement and the choice is easy: A correction officer and a police officer **do have** a lot in common.

8. There **are** a police officer at the front door and two reporters at the back. Watch out for inverted clauses that begin with *there*. In this sentence, *two reporters* requires the use of the plural *are*. Note that if proper grammar sounds awkward to you, you can always re-write the sentence: *There are two reporters at the back door and a police officer at the front.*

9. Everybody on the 4-12 shift has satisfied **his** in-service training requirement. Use a singular pronoun when the antecedent is everybody, everyone, everything, anyone, anybody, anything, someone, somebody, something, no one, and nobody.

10. In those days there **were** only 35 officers on the Department and two dispatchers. The subject, *35 officers*, requires the plural *were*.

11. The sum and substance of the class **was** "proper preparation." Here's an exception to the compound subject rule. A singular verb should be used when two or more subjects connected by *and* refer to the same person or thing, for example, *Our secretary and treasurer is* John Jones. In this item, the subject, *The sum and substance*, is singular, requiring use of the word *was*.

12. The long and short of it **is** that you must study to do well. As in the last question, this subject, *The long and short of it*, is singular.

13. A friend and colleague of mine **is** in charge of the Detective Bureau. Similarly, *friend and colleague* is a singular subject.

14. My sergeant, as well as my lieutenant, **expects** that it will be done by the end of the day. The subject, *My sergeant*, requires a singular verb. Although the sentence is talking about two people, *my sergeant and my lieutenant*, the prepositional phrase, *as well as my lieutenant*, forecloses the use of a plural verb. Prepositions such as *together with, along with, in addition to,* or *as well as*, do not perform the same job as the conjunction and. Remember, the object of a preposition cannot be the subject of a verb.

15. Tom, as well as Sam, **prefers** coffee to tea. As in the last item, the singular subject, *Tom*, requires a singular verb.

16. The strength of the platoon, along with the high morale, **has** made working here very pleasant. As in the last two items, the singular subject, *strength* requires a singular verb.

17. None of the officers completed **his** assignment. Use a singular pronoun when the antecedent is, as here, "none." Also use a singular pronoun when the antecedent is no one, nobody, either, neither, each, another, one, person, man, woman, or kind.

18. Officer Robinson is the only one of the five day shift officers who **have** entered the weight lifting competition who **is** likely to win. Here, the antecedent of the first *who* is the plural *officers*. Therefore, *who* is plural and the correct verb is *have*. But the antecedent of the second *who* is *one* (and the antecedent of *one* is Robinson), and so the verb in this clause must be the singular *is*.

19. Either the captain or the lieutenant **is** responsible for the completion of the crime statistics. The singular *lieutenant* is the subject of the verb.

20. The number of articles about sexual scandal in government written by members of the media during the Clinton administration **seems** to grow larger every month. The singular *The number* is the subject.

Notes

The proper use of the English language is a must for Effective Law Enforcement Reporting. As one commentator observed, "I know you believe you understand what you think I had written, but I'm not sure you realize that what you read is not what I meant to write." The following exercises are designed to test your ability to identify errors of standard written English as they appear in sentences.

Directions:

For the next 11 items, a portion of a sentence is underlined. Choices for rephrasing the underlined part follow each sentence. Choice (a) merely repeats the original; the other choices are different. If choice (a) is better than the alternatives, choose (a); if not, choose one of the others. For each item, ask yourself whether the requirements of standard written English have been met. Choose an expression that states what needs to be stated in a clear, effective, concise and straightforward way; not in an awkward or ambiguous way. Pay attention to word selection, grammar, sentence construction, and punctuation. If an answer choice changes the meaning of the original sentence, do not select it.

GO ON TO THE NEXT PAGE.

1. Sexual harassment is defined not only <u>as physical assaults of a sexual nature, but also how this harassment can include unwanted sexual advances, propositions or other sexual comments.</u>

    (a) as physical assaults of a sexual nature, but also how this harassment can include unwanted sexual advances, propositions or other sexual comments.

    (b) as physical assaults of a sexual nature, but also how this harassment can be punished.

    (c) as physical assaults of a sexual nature, but also including methods for combating unwanted sexual advances, propositions or other sexual comments.

    (d) as physical assaults of a sexual nature but also as unwanted sexual advances, propositions or other sexual comments.

2. Listening to a female officer being subjected to sexually oriented noises, remarks and jokes <u>by a supervisor, requires prompt reporting of such sexual harassment as a matter of policy.</u>

    (a) by a supervisor, requires prompt reporting of such sexual harassment as a matter of policy.

    (b) by a supervisor, suggests to all that the sexual harassment must be reported by policy.

    (c) by a supervisor, I promptly reported the sexual harassment pursuant to policy.

    (d) by a supervisor, prompts the need for policy reporting of the sexual harassment.

3. In order to ensure the integrity of the work environment, all personnel in a supervisory or management function <u>are required to ensure adherence to and compliance with this Department's sexual harassment policy.</u>

    (a) are required to ensure adherence to and compliance with this Department's sexual harassment policy.

    (b) is to ensure adherence to and compliance with this Department's sexual harassment policy.

    (c) may require adherence to and compliance with this Department's sexual harassment policy.

    (d) are required to adhere strictly to this Department's sexual harassment policy.

GO ON TO THE NEXT PAGE.

4. When you file a sexual harassment complaint, <u>it may be filed either concurrently or sequentially with the internal affairs unit, the supervisors in the employee's chain of command or in other forums,</u> such as the courts, the Division on Civil Rights or the Equal Employment Opportunity Commission.

    (a) it may be filed either concurrently or sequentially with the internal affairs unit, the supervisors in the employee's chain of command or in other forums,

    (b) you may file it either concurrently or sequentially with the internal affairs unit, the supervisors in the employee's chain of command or in other forums,

    (c) it must be filed concurrently through the internal affairs unit, the supervisors in the employee's chain of command, then in other forums,

    (d) the aggrieved employee may file it concurrently or sequentially with the internal affairs unit, the supervisors in the employee's chain of command or in other forums,

5. Any <u>employee that is subjected to sexual harassment is</u> encouraged, whether directly or through a third party, to notify the alleged harasser that the behavior in question is offensive and unwelcome.

    (a) employee that is subjected to sexual harassment is

    (b) employee who is subjected to sexual harassment is

    (c) employee which witnesses sexual harassment is

    (d) employee subjected to sexual harassment may

6. "Quid Pro Quo" sexual <u>harassment occur when a supervisor and</u> management level employee conditions continued employment or further job benefits on sexual favors by a subordinate employee.

    (a) harassment occur when a supervisor and

    (b) harassment occurs when a supervisor and

    (c) harassment occurs when a supervisor or

    (d) harassment may occur when a supervisor or

GO ON TO THE NEXT PAGE.

7. "Hostile Work Environment" or "Environmental" sexual harassment occurs when a supervisor <u>or co-worker's sexually- or gender-based conduct</u> has the effect of unreasonably interfering with an employee's work performance <u>or has the effect of creating an intimidating, hostile, or offensive work environment.</u>

(a) or co-worker's sexually- or gender-based conduct...or has the effect of creating an intimidating, hostile, or offensive work environment.

(b) or co-worker's sexual or gender-based conduct...or an intimidating, hostile, or offensive work environment.

(c) and co-worker's sexually and gender-based conduct...or has the effect of creating an intimidating, hostile, or offensive work environment.

(d) or co-worker's sexual/gender conduct...or creates an intimidating, hostile, or offensive work environment.

8. The picture of the sexually explicit Playboy centerfold, displayed just outside the men's locker <u>room was the one belonging to this officer.</u>

(a) room was the one belonging to this officer.

(b) room was the item that belonged to this officer.

(c) room was mine.

(d) room was my property.

9. The rigors of a police officer's job often demand <u>stamina, persistence, and having great patience.</u>

(a) stamina, persistence, and having great patience.

(b) stamina, persistence, and great patience.

(c) that a person has stamina, persistence, and patience.

(d) having stamina, being persistent, and having patience.

GO ON TO THE NEXT PAGE.

10. Rushing to avoid being late, <u>Jim's head collided with the locker door</u> <u>which was open.</u>

(a) Jim's head collided with the locker door which was open.

(b) Jim's head hit the open locker door.

(c) Jim's head collided with the open locker door.

(d) Jim hit his head on the open locker door.

11. The reason the sergeant cannot attend is <u>because he had a death in</u> <u>the family.</u>

(a) because he had a death in the family.

(b) that he lost a loved family member.

(c) on account of he had a death in the family.

(d) that he had a death in the family.

GO ON TO THE NEXT PAGE.

Effective Law Enforcement Report Writing

Directions:
Each of the sentences set forth below may contain an error in grammar, usage, idiom (nonstandard usage / vocabulary natural to a specific group of people), or diction (word choice). You are to fill in the letter (ⓐ, ⓑ, ⓒ, or ⓓ) of the part of the sentence which is incorrect. If no part of the sentence is incorrect, fill in letter ⓔ.

12. Each officer on the second and **third** shift **at the department** gave
ⓐ   ⓑ

their reasons **for disagreeing** with the policy. **No error.**
ⓒ   ⓓ   ⓔ

13. The **threatening** group of new arrivals, first **seen** by the academy
ⓐ   ⓑ

instructors, **were** amused by all **who** watched them. **No error.**
ⓒ   ⓓ   ⓔ

14. John's diligence **in studying every night** allowed him to score
ⓐ

high on his promotional exam, to gain the respect **of his peers**,
ⓑ   ⓒ

and **promotion** to the next rank. **No error.**
ⓓ   ⓔ

15. **Compromising over** a number of delicate issues, the members
ⓐ

of the contract negotiation team successfully resolved **their**
ⓑ   ⓒ   ⓓ

problems. **No error.**
ⓔ

16. **Despite** his late start, Williams is the officer **whom** I think **is** most
ⓐ   ⓑ   ⓒ

likely to score the highest on the **promotional** exam. **No error.**
ⓓ   ⓔ

17. **Most** all the officers and supervisors on the shift **are briefed**
ⓐ   ⓑ

just before starting their tour of duty; the lieutenants, **of course**,
ⓒ   ⓓ

are an exception. **No error.**
ⓔ

GO ON TO THE NEXT PAGE.

18. The **rise** in mandatory sentencing, together with the
      ⓐ

increase in the crime rate, **have effected** a significant increase in
          ⓑ   ⓒ

prison overcrowding in this State. **No error.**
     ⓓ   ⓔ

19. **The number of** juvenile offenders in this State **was** larger than
       ⓐ   ⓑ

adult women, but it was not as large as the number of **adult men**.
   ⓒ   ⓓ

No error.
  ⓔ

20. The sharpshooters of the department, **which** frequently **provide** to
                       ⓐ   ⓑ

assist officers in the field, **are expected** to be given **specialized**
               ⓒ   ⓓ

training this week. **No error.**
         ⓔ

21. The increasing number **of crimes** that **carry** stiff penalties **should**
             ⓐ   ⓑ   ⓒ

act as a general deterrent and be **of significant concern** to
                       ⓓ

criminals. **No error.**
     ⓔ

22. Everybody assigned to training at the academy **have been effected**
                             ⓐ   ⓑ

in some way by the severe snowstorm, but there is **not yet** any
                               ⓒ

certainty as to **just what** the full extent of problem will be. **No error.**
          ⓓ   ⓔ

23. **From a public** safety standpoint, Corrections and Policing **together**
     ⓐ   ⓑ

are critical components of an **ever-changing** Criminal Justice
ⓒ   ⓓ

System. **No error.**
       ⓔ

GO ON TO THE NEXT PAGE.

Directions:

This exercise continues to test your ability to identify errors related to English usage and punctuation. You will be given a complete paragraph to read and analyze. You are to determine if any part of any sentence is incorrect, and then you are to correct it, if necessary, by choosing from among several choices. If the bold part is correct and makes sense with the rest of the passage, choose the answer that says "NO CHANGE."

24. Furthering one's goals may require more effort than one had originally intended. Yet, a man or woman may underestimate **their** capacity for work when setting out to accomplish some task.

24. (a) NO CHANGE.
    (b) its
    (c) ones'
    (d) his or her

25. When preparing for a promotional exam, you should insure that the following items are included in your study **materials; pens** and pencils, note paper, highlighters, and all the books and policies that relate to the position sought.

25. (a) NO CHANGE.
    (b) materials, pens
    (c) materials: pens
    (d) materials. Pens

26. Earning a **promotion it seems is a goal** worth pursuing.

26. (a) NO CHANGE
    (b) promotion, it seems is a goal
    (c) promotion it seems, is a goal
    (d) promotion, it seems, is a goal

GO ON TO THE NEXT PAGE.

27. How else can we explain the promotional exam preparation battle being waged between some officers over the best kind of **course to attend. If** you

27. (a) NO CHANGE
(b) course to attend? If
(c) course to attend; if
(d) course to attend! If

28. are up for promotion, you know what we are talking about. Today, alongside those **tried trusty and true** preparation courses that officers have relied on in the past, are many fly-by-night courses not worth attending.

28. (a) NO CHANGE
(b) tried, trusty, and true
(c) tried trusty, and true
(d) tried, trusty and true,

29. The folks who run these courses contend that cheaper is **better— those officers who are that are on a budget—** because

29. (a) NO CHANGE
(b) better, at least for at least, for those officers on a budget—
(c) better—at least for those officers who are on a budget—
(d) better, at least, for those officers, who are on a budget,

30. the preparation is the **same; the** same information is covered; and the time involved is not as great. This, however, is far from the truth.

30. (a) NO CHANGE
(b) same the
(c) same, the
(d) same—the

END OF EXERCISE

1. (d) The *not only...but also* should both be followed by a parallel construction, *as*, and a (modified) noun. In addition, there is no need for a comma before the word *but*. A comma should not separate correlative pairs, such as *both...and*, *neither...nor*, *either...or*, and *not only...but also*.

2. (c) Participles are verb forms generally ending in *ing* or *ed*. When a participle functions as an adjective, it should modify a noun or pronoun. If a writer does not attach a participial phrase to a word in a sentence, or if he or she attaches it to the wrong word, the participle is left "dangling." In this item, only choice (c) supplies an appropriate word, I, for the dangling participle (*Listening to the female officer...*) to modify.

3. (a) Since *personnel* is plural, the verb must be *are*.

4. (b) Since the sentence begins with *you*, the subject of the main clause should also be *you*.

5. (b) Given a choice among *who*, *which*, or *that*, use *who* when the antecedent is a single human being (*the man who*, or *John Smith, who*, or *the employee who*) or a group thought of as individuals (*the lawmakers who, the players who, the jurors who*). Use *that* or *which* for a group thought of as a group (the senate that; the squad, which, the shift that. Answer (d) changes the meaning of the sentence.

6. (c) The singular subject, *sexual harassment*, requires a singular verb, *occurs*. Also, the word *"or"* is more correct because the word *"and"* incorrectly suggests that the activity could only occur if BOTH a supervisor and a management level employee engage in the activity. Answer (d) changes the meaning of the sentence.

7. (a) This is correct as written. Answer (b) is wrong because the two compound adjectives modifying conduct should appear as: *sexually-based* or *gender-based*. The shorter version is, however, proper. Given the choice between two grammatically correct sentences whose meaning is the same, you should choose the shorter, more concise version, BUT be sure that there are no necessary words missing. In the second clause here, the shorter version changes the meaning of the definition. Answer (c) is wrong because the word *and* changes the meaning of the definition to require a supervisor *and* a co-worker to jointly engage in the prohibited conduct. Answer (d) also changes the meaning of the sentence.

8. (c) This is the most direct and natural way of saying this. The other answers are artificial and too long.

9. (b) In this question, the underlined part contains a *faulty parallelism*. The last item in the series should not be preceded by the word *"having"* but should be in the same form as *"stamina"* and *"persistence."* By omitting the word *"great,"* choices (c) and (d) slightly change the meaning of the original and also have errors of parallelism.

10. (d) This sentence begins with an *"-ing"* phrase, which modifies what immediately follows the comma. In the original, Jim's head follows the modifying phrase. Was Jim's head doing the rushing? Clearly not. The sentence should read, *"Rushing to avoid being late, Jim hit his head…"*. Jim should follow the modifying phrase because he, not his head, was doing the rushing.

11. (d) With the phrase *"The reason…is"*, you must use the pronoun *"that,"* not the conjunction *"because."* Choice (d) is preferable to choice (b) because of the two present tenses. Choice (b) shifts from present to past tense.

12. (c) In this item, *"Each officer"* is not underlined, so the subject of the sentence is singular. Therefore, *there* is not correct. It should be *his* to agree with the singular subject.

13. (c) Other agreement errors in standard written English may include *subject-verb errors* such as in this question. Since the subject of the sentence is *"group"* (singular), the verb must also be singular—*"was."*

14. (d) Other errors may include *faulty parallelism*. This is generally tested by giving you items in a series with one part of the series not in the same form (*not parallel*) as the other parts. In this question, the final part of the series is not in the same form as the first two parts. It should read…*"to earn promotion,"* or *"to obtain a promotion,"* so that it parallels the form of the other items in the series— *"to score"* and *"to gain."*

15. (a) This question involves an error in *idiom* (nonstandard usage of a word or phrase). The expression *"compromising over"* is unidiomatic. It should be *"compromising on."* Part (a) is not correct standard written English and therefore should be selected as the correct answer.

16. (b) The *"whom"* should be *"who,"* the subject of the clause *"who is most likely to score the highest on the promotional exam."* The *"I think"* is merely parenthetical. Use **whom** when the word is the **object** of a sentence or clause, for example, "To **whom** it may concern…."

17. (a) The adverb *"almost"* should be used to modify the adjective *"all."*

18. (b) The subject *"rise"* is singular. Therefore, the correct verb is *"has effected."* The use of the prepositional phrase, *"together with"* does not make the subject plural.

19. (c) The comparison here should be between *"the number of juvenile offenders"* and *"the number of adult women."*

20. (a) Since the *"sharpshooters"* are humans, the pronoun *who* not *which* should be used. You might be tempted to choose (b) reasoning that the sentence should read... *the department which frequently provides*...however, this choice would not use the appropriate diction, suggesting that a *"department"* (an inanimate thing) could provide something frequently.

21. (b) The singular word—*"number"*— is the subject; as a result, the verb should also be singular, *"carries."*

22. (a) The singular word *"Everybody"* should be followed by the singular verb *"has been."*

23. (e) The sentence is correct as written.

24. (d) This question involves "pronoun agreement." As a general rule, when two or more antecedents are joined by *"or"* or *"nor"* the pronoun should agree with the nearer antecedent. Since the nearest antecedent in this item is singular (*woman*), the pronoun should also be singular, choice (d) *"his or her."* For another example of this rule, note the following: "Neither the mother nor the *sons* brought *their* cars."

25. (c) The list of study materials should be introduced with a colon.

26. (d) The phrase *"it seems"* is parenthetical and should be set off by two commas.

27. (b) The sentence is a question.

28. (b) These items are in a series and should be set off by commas.

29. (c) The dashes set off the interrupting phrase. One could use commas instead of dashes, but not one comma and one dash as in choice (b) No commas are needed after *least* and *those.*

30. (a) The semicolon here divides the parts of a series.

Notes

Directions:
This exercise continues to test your ability to identify errors related to standard written English as they appear in sentences. Each of the sentences set forth below may contain an error in grammar, usage, idiom (nonstandard usage / vocabulary natural to a specific group or people), or diction (word choice). Fill in the letter (ⓐ, ⓑ, ⓒ, or ⓓ) of the part of the sentence which is incorrect. If no part of the sentence if incorrect, fill in letter E.

1. The **imposing** group of superior officers first **encountered** by the
    ⓐ   ⓑ

    new recruits **were** immediately respected by all **who** met them.
                   ⓒ   ⓓ

    No Error.
    ⓔ

2. **Most** all the applicants for the position **are sent** complete
    ⓐ   ⓑ

    information packets; the applicants **who** are reapplying are an
                                       ⓒ

    exception because they **already** have received a packet. **No Error.**
                      ⓓ   ⓔ

3. Each supervisor on the second and third shift **at the** jail gave **their**
                                                ⓐ   ⓑ

    opinion **regarding** the new **policies. No Error.**
                   ⓒ   ⓓ   ⓔ

GO ON TO THE NEXT PAGE.

4. The number of new applicants for the position of sergeant **were**
ⓐ
larger than **last year**, but **it** was not **nearly** as large as the number
ⓑ   ⓒ   ⓓ
of applicants the first year. **No Error.**
ⓔ

5. The inmates of the prison **which** complain of mistreatment and
ⓐ
poor conditions are **expected** to be given a hearing **before** the
ⓑ   ⓒ   ⓓ
Civilian Review Board. **No Error.**
ⓔ

6. The **ever-growing** group of citizens **who** support local law
ⓐ   ⓑ
enforcement **is** a result of **more favorable** television and print
ⓒ   ⓓ
coverage. **No Error.**
ⓔ

7. Twelve recruits **have been assigned** to attend the sensitivity
ⓐ
training seminar, and each of the recruits **have been given** an
ⓑ
information packet **to use** during the **training** seminar. **No Error.**
ⓒ   ⓓ   ⓔ

8. **Of the three** officers recognized for bravery and heroic action,
ⓐ
Officer Green **was** the **more decorated**, **having received** two
ⓑ   ⓒ   ⓓ
previous meritorious citations. **No Error.**
ⓔ

9. **Discussing** a number of delicate issues, the members of the **union's**
ⓐ   ⓑ
negotiation team successfully **resolved** all of **there** major issues.
ⓒ   ⓓ
No Error.
ⓔ

GO ON TO THE NEXT PAGE.

10. Each of the female officers **assigned** to the graveyard shift gave **their**
ⓐ ⓑ
reasons **for wanting to** be **reassigned** to another shift. **No Error.**
ⓒ ⓓ ⓔ

11. **Settling over** many of **their** complaints, the members of the
ⓐ ⓑ
negotiation team for the **inmates** were **thanked** for their time and
ⓒ ⓓ
effort. **No Error.**
ⓔ

12. The twelve **volunteer** members of the Civilian Review Board **were**
ⓐ ⓑ
highly commended for **their** dedication, effort, and
ⓒ
patiently considering all complaints. **No Error.**
ⓓ ⓔ

13. Each **female** candidate on the list of new recruits gave **their** reasons
ⓐ ⓑ
for wanting to join the force and **become** part of the
ⓒ ⓓ
community-based solution. **No Error.**
ⓔ

14. This pool of female candidates, first **interviewed** by the captain,
ⓐ
and then by several lieutenants, **were praised** highly for **its** depth
ⓑ ⓒ ⓓ
and quality. **No Error.**
ⓔ

15. The police training **program, conducted** by the State,
ⓐ ⓑ
was stimulating and **a challenge. No Error.**
ⓒ ⓓ ⓔ

16. **Being that** there **was** a very large number of highly detailed reports
ⓐ ⓑ
to read and it was already **past** midnight, the Civilian Review Board
ⓒ
adjourned for the evening. **No Error.**
ⓓ ⓔ

GO ON TO THE NEXT PAGE.

17. This **year's** representative **is** Jim Wade; the next representative will be
   ⓐ   ⓑ
   whoever the delegates **elect** at the convention in January. **No Error**.
   ⓒ   ⓓ   ⓔ

18. The **rookie** trooper gave the man a ticket for **going** eight miles an
   ⓐ   ⓑ
   hour over the speed limit; **subsequently** his superior officer told the
   ⓒ
   trooper that he **should have left** the man go with a warning.
   ⓓ
   No Error.
   ⓔ

19. The mayor of the city, together with the town council,

   has been dealing with the problem of **teenage** vandalism in order
   ⓐ   ⓑ
   to try **to lessen** the **number** of complaints from irate citizens.
   ⓒ   ⓓ
   No Error.
   ⓔ

20. The information **obtained from** a civilian eyewitness is **usually** less
   ⓐ   ⓑ
   accurate than **from** a trained officer. **No Error**.
   ⓒ   ⓓ   ⓔ

21. When a **prospective** employer **is interviewing** you, one of the first
   ⓐ   ⓑ
   things **they** will ask about is previous job experience and
   ⓒ
   training. **No Error**.
   ⓓ   ⓔ

22. A **non-aggressive** attitude and respect **both are** important
   ⓐ   ⓑ
   to diffusing a potentially inflammatory situation and to gaining
   ⓒ
   overall respect. **No Error**.
   ⓓ   ⓔ

GO ON TO THE NEXT PAGE.

23. The apprehended suspect made some flippant remark and **tries**
    (a)
to **rush off** down the hall and out the door, **only** to be stopped in
    (b)   (c)
his tracks by the **securely locked** door. **No Error.**
                        (d)   (e)

24. The community-based resource council, **working** closely with the
                                              (a)
police, **established** an outreach guideline that **is** now **being used**
        (b)   (c)   (d)
in several cities. **No Error.**
                    (e)

25. A healthy diet and moderate exercise **is** of **utmost** importance for
                                             (a)   (b)
us all; however, not enough Americans realize **their** importance.
(c)   (d)
No Error.
    (e)

26. **When** we are not working, many of us are watching television,
        (a)
surfing the internet, or **we eat** junk food; all of **which** helps to make
                          (b)   (c)
us a nation of overweight citizens. **No Error.**
(d)   (e)

27. The Police Athletic League warehouse stocks balls, bats, rackets,

helmets, pads, bases, **and etc.**, that **may** be used by **any** person or
                      (a)   (b)   (c)
group when they **are used** for an activity sanctioned by the Police
                (d)
Athletic League. **No Error.**
                  (e)

28. **After** thirty years on the force, the officer **had** an unblemished
        (a)   (b)
and **was known** as one of those **who** neither the criminals nor
    (c)   (d)
politicians could influence. **No Error.**
                              (e)

GO ON TO THE NEXT PAGE.

29. The suspect admitted it was **him** the witness **had seen** in front of
ⓐ   ⓑ

the drugstore, but **insisted** he had nothing to do with **its** robbery
ⓒ   ⓓ

last night. **No Error.**
ⓔ

30. The local NAACP, **together with** several **other** groups, **is planning**
ⓐ   ⓑ   ⓒ

a large conference in **our** city. **No Error.**
ⓓ   ⓔ

31. Both the mayor and the town council **were** at the funeral and
ⓐ

could see plainly how the sudden death of **their** captain **effected**
ⓑ   ⓒ   ⓓ

the entire department. **No Error.**
ⓔ

32. **While** the detective found the younger girl to be the **most**
ⓐ   ⓑ

cooperative of the two witnesses, he **decided** the second witness
ⓒ

was more likely telling the truth and continued **to concentrate** on
ⓓ

questioning her. **No Error.**
ⓔ

33. I chased the overweight suspect up four flights of steps and **caught**
ⓐ

him on the fifth-floor landing, **where** he **was complaining** that he
ⓑ   ⓒ

couldn't **hardly** breathe and asked me to call an ambulance.
ⓓ

No Error.
ⓔ

34. The increasing number of crimes in our neighborhood **are causing**
ⓐ

many residents **to install** new safety devices around **their** houses
ⓑ   ⓒ

and to insist on more police patrols during **each** shift. **No Error.**
ⓓ   ⓔ

GO ON TO THE NEXT PAGE.

Directions:
The following items continue to test your knowledge of standard written English. For these items, you are to choose the BEST of the given versions of the sentence presented. If the original sentence most fully meets the requirements of correct English grammar and usage, choice (a), which merely repeats the underlined portion, should be selected. If the underlined portion is incorrect, awkward, or ambiguous, choose the version that BEST corrects it and retains the original meaning of the underlined portion.

35. The suspect was feeling <u>sick, nauseous, and she was weak.</u>

   (a) sick, nauseous, and she was weak.

   (b) sickly, nauseous, and she was weak.

   (c) sick, nauseous, and weak.

   (d) sickly, nauseated, and weak.

   (e) sickly, nauseous, and weakly.

36. Two meetings have been held <u>to make arrangements for a return bout in the office of the State Athletic Commission.</u>

   (a) to make arrangements for a return bout in the office of the State Athletic Commission.

   (b) making arrangements for a return bout in the office of the State Athletic Commission.

   (c) to make arrangements in the office of the State Athletic Commission for a return bout.

   (d) in the office of the State Athletic Commission to make arrangements for a return bout.

   (e) arranging a return bout in the office of the State Athletic Commission.

37. The reason he refused to go was <u>because he had no money.</u>

   (a) because he had no money.

   (b) that he had no money.

   (c) because he hadn't any money.

   (d) that he was broke.

   (e) because of the fact that he had no money.

GO ON TO THE NEXT PAGE.

38. The mother cried <u>at the arraignment of her son hysterically.</u>

    (a) at the arraignment of her son hysterically.

    (b) at her son's arraignment hysterically.

    (c) in hysteria at her son's arraignment.

    (d) at the arraignment hysterically her son.

    (e) hysterically at her son's arraignment.

39. Everyone has intelligence, but <u>he or she must develop it.</u>

    (a) he or she must develop it.

    (b) where they can develop it.

    (c) but they must develop it.

    (d) but must develop them.

    (e) where he or she must develop it.

40. Police Athletic Leagues need additional funding <u>and to get resources.</u>

    (a) and to get resources.

    (b) and resources must be added.

    (c) and resources.

    (d) and get resources.

    (e) and need more resources.

41. The warden was extremely aggravated by <u>his prisoner yelling</u> all night.

    (a) his prisoner yelling

    (b) him prisoner yelling

    (c) his prisoner's yelling

    (d) his prisoners' yelling

    (e) the yelling of his prisoner's

GO ON TO THE NEXT PAGE.

42. It was June 10 <u>when the job opening is posted</u> at work.

    (a) when the job opening is posted

    (b) when the job opening was posted

    (c) where the job opening has been posted

    (d) where the job opening was posted

    (e) as the job opening is posted

43. Neither the officers nor their supervisor <u>are giving</u> any information about the suspect they arrested last night.

    (a) are giving

    (b) giving

    (c) is giving

    (d) give

    (e) were giving

44. Our city can be a stimulating place for families to live <u>and rear their children.</u>

    (a) and rear their children.

    (b) and rear its children.

    (c) and rear there children.

    (d) to rear its children.

    (e) and their children are reared.

45. Playing the guitar, <u>the prisoners were entertained by Johnny Cash.</u>

    (a) the prisoners were entertained by Johnny Cash.

    (b) the prisoners was entertained by Johnny Cash.

    (c) the prisoners entertained by Johnny Cash.

    (d) Johnny Cash entertaining the prisoners.

    (e) Johnny Cash entertained the prisoners.

END OF EXERCISE

1. (c) For proper subject-verb agreement, the singular subject *group* requires the singular verb *was*.

2. (a) *Most*, a noun, should be replaced with the adverb *Almost*, which would modify *all*.

3. (b) For proper pronoun agreement, the singular antecedent *Each* (as in *Each one…gave*) requires the singular pronoun *his*.

4. (a) For proper subject-verb agreement, the singular subject *number* requires the singular verb *was*.

5. (a) The word *which* refers to things. It should be replaced with *who* which refers to people, here, *inmates*.

6. (e) This sentence is correct as written.

7. (b) For proper subject-verb agreement, the singular subject *each* requires the singular verb form *has been*.

8. (c) For the proper use of a comparative adjective here, use *most decorated*. When comparing two items, use *more*; when comparing more than two items, use *most*.

9. (d) This is a spelling error. Here, *members* requires the use of *their*.

10. (b) Use a singular pronoun when the antecedent is singular. Here, *each* requires the use of *her*.

11. (a) This is an example of a non-standard usage. The correct language should be: *Settling* many of their complaints, the members….

12. (d) For the proper use of parallel construction, the phrase should read:…commended for their dedication, effort, and *patient consideration* of all complaints.

13. (b) For proper pronoun agreement, the singular antecedent *Each* (as in *Each one…gave*) requires the singular pronoun *her*.

14. (c) For proper subject-verb agreement, the singular subject *pool* requires the singular verb *was*.

15. (d) For proper parallel construction, adjectives should be paralleled by adjectives, nouns by nouns, dependent clauses by dependent clauses, and so on. This item contains an obvious error in parallelism: The police training program, conducted by the State, was *stimulating* and a *challenge*. (Adjective and noun.) To correct the error: The police training program was *stimulating* and *challenging*. (Two adjectives).

16. (a) This is an example of non-standard usage. *Being that* should not be used in place of *since* or *because*.

17. (c) The proper pronoun is *whomever*. Use *who* whenever *he, she, they, I,* or *we* could be substituted in the *who* clause, for example, *Who called* the police? *Who shall* I say is calling. We will pick *whoever meets* the qualifications. Use *whom* whenever *him, her, them, me,* or *us* could be substituted as the object of the verb or as the object of a preposition in the *whom* clause, for example, *To whom were* you speaking. *To whom* it may concern…. They will promote *whomever they choose*.

18. (d) Here is another example of non-standard usage. The phrase should read, *should have let*….

19. (e) This sentence is correct as written. The intervening phrase, *together with the town council*, does not change the fact the subject, *mayor*, is singular.

20. (d) For proper parallel construction, the phrase should read:...*is usually less accurate than the information obtained from a trained officer.*

21. (c) For proper pronoun agreement, the singular antecedent, *prospective employer*, requires the singular pronoun *he* or *she*.

22. (b) Proper usage requires that the phrase read:...*attitude and respect are both important....*

23. (a) This sentence presents an error in verb tense. To correct:... *suspect made...and tried....*

24. (e) This sentence is correct as written.

25. (a) For proper subject-verb agreement, the plural (compound) subject, *diet and moderate exercise*, requires the plural verb form *are*.

26. (b) For proper parallel construction, the phrase should read:...*many of us are watching...surfing...or eating....*

27. (a) The word *etc.* means "*and* other things." Therefore, there is no need for the word *and* here.

28. (d) The proper pronoun is *whom*, the object of the verb form *could influence*. Use *whom* whenever *him, her, them, me,* or *us* could be substituted as the object of the verb.

29. (a) The proper pronoun should be *he*.

30. (e) This sentence is correct as written.

31. (d) This sentence contains an error in word choice. To correct:...*the sudden death of their captain affected the entire department*. Note that the word *affect* is a verb that means "to influence, change, or assume." In psychology, *affect* is used as a noun meaning "feeling or emotion." *Effect*, on the other hand, can be either a verb meaning "to bring about," or a noun meaning "result" or "impression." Here are a few more examples: *The Chief needs to analyze the effects (results) of this new procedure. We need to analyze the affects (emotions) produced by the recent shooting. Which defensive tactic technique is effective (capable of producing the desired results)? The Victim-Witness Unit deals with the affective (emotional) factors first.*

32. (b) When comparing two things, use *more*. When comparing more than two things, use *most*. To correct: *While the detective found the younger girl to be the more cooperative of the two witnesses, he decided....*

33. (d) As written, the sentence contains an improper "double negative." Since *hardly* is a negative, the phrase *couldn't hardly* suggests the opposite of what was intended. To correct:...*he was complaining that he couldn't breathe....*

34. (a) For proper subject-verb agreement, the singular subject *number* requires the singular verb form, *is causing*.

35. (c) For proper parallel construction, adjectives should be paralleled by adjectives, nouns by nouns, dependent clauses by dependent clauses, and so on. In this item, three adjectives should be used (*sick*, *nauseous*, and *weak*).

36. (d) For clarity, the phrase *in the office of the State Athletic Commission* should be placed right after the word it modifies, *held*.

37. (b) With the phrase, *The reason...*, the pronoun *that* should be used, not the conjunction *because*. Note that choice (d) is not correct due to the use of the slang term, *broke*.

38. (e) The adverb *hysterically* should be next to the word it modifies, *cried*.

39. (a) This sentence is correct as written.

40. (c) For parallel construction,....*Leagues need...funding and resources.*

41. (c) Use the possessive case to show ownership and other relationships. An apostrophe alone or an apostrophe and an *s* is the sign of the possessive. For the correct use of the possessive case in this item, add the apostrophe, *prisoner's* yelling.

42. (b) To correct the error in verb tense, use...opening *was* posted....

43. (c) For proper subject-verb agreement, when two subjects are joined by *or* or *nor*, the verb should agree with the subject that is nearer to the verb; here, *supervisor*.

44. (a) This sentence is correct as written.

45. (e) The modifier in this sentence is misplaced. It should read: *Playing the guitar, Johnny Cash entertained....*

The following exercises continue to test your knowledge of standard written English.

Directions:

For questions 1 through 10, read the following passage. You are being tested on your ability to identify errors of standard written English as they appear in sentences. Each numbered portion of the sentences may contain an error in grammar, punctuation, usage, or diction (word choice). Choose the best of the four different versions that follow the passage. If the numbered part of the original sentence meets the requirements of correct and effective English, choose choice (a), which merely repeats the underlined portion. If the underlined portion is incorrect, awkward, or ambiguous, you must choose the version that best corrects it and retains the meaning of the original bold phrase.

GO ON TO THE NEXT PAGE.

155

Its getting much easier to buy a **home these days. It use to be** more
① ② ③
difficult and much more expensive to **buy yourself a home** because
④
financing was not always readily available. In the past, when financing

was available, home buyers were required to invest a very large down

payment. **Because it took** too much of a family's earnings and savings
⑤
to buy a home. Most people understand that it **takes a lot** out of their
⑥
monthly income to maintain the mortgage. Today, buying a home still

requires a down payment of **money but** because many banks have
⑦
a surplus supply of homes to sell due to foreclosures, they are more
⑧
willing to sell without requiring an extraordinarily large down

payment. In addition, since so many real estate agencies have so

many homes that **the home-buying public has not yet seen fit to buy**,
⑨
they are more willing to deal. Therefore, to increase **sales, the** real estate
⑩
agents and lending institutions are now selling homes without

requiring much of a down payment.

1. (a) Its getting
   (b) It's getting
   (c) It will get
   (d) Its gonna get

2. (a) home these days
   (b) home for days
   (c) home today
   (d) home this day

GO ON TO THE NEXT PAGE.

3. (a) It use to be
    (b) It had been
    (c) It used to be
    (d) It was

4. (a) buy yourself a home
    (b) buy one's self a home
    (c) buy you a home
    (d) buy the family a home

5. (a) Because it took
    (b) It took
    (c) It may take
    (d) On account of it took

6. (a) takes a lot
    (b) takes allot
    (c) takes a lot
    (d) takes much

7. (a) money but
    (b) funds yet
    (c) money for
    (d) money, but

8. (a) a surplus supply of homes
    (b) a surplus volume of homes
    (c) too many homes
    (d) a great deal in surplus of homes

9. (a) the home-buying public has not yet seen fit to buy
    (b) the public isn't ready to buy yet
    (c) the home-buying public do not really like
    (d) are not very appealing to the average person

10. (a) sales, the
    (b) sales the
    (c) sales. The
    (d) sales: the

END OF EXERCISE

It is critical to note that you are looking for errors in standard written English. It is also helpful to remember that the portions of the sentence that are not underlined are correct. You should try to use the parts which are not underlined to help determine which underlined portion may be wrong.

1.   (b)   It's getting. (This is a contraction for "It is.")

2.   (a)   home these days

3.   (c)   It used to be

4.   (a)   buy yourself a home

5.   (b)   It took

6.   (a)   takes a lot

7.   (d)   money, but

8.   (c)   too many homes (*Keep it Short and Simple*)

9.   (b)   the public isn't ready to buy yet

10. (a)   sales, the

Directions:

Questions 1 through 11 continue to test you on your ability to identify errors of standard written English as they appear in sentences. As before, choose the best of the four different versions that follow the passage. If the numbered part of the original sentence meets the requirements of correct and effective English, choose choice (a), which merely repeats the underlined portion. If the bold portion is incorrect, awkward, or ambiguous, you must choose the version that best corrects it and retains the meaning of the original bold phrase.

GO ON TO THE NEXT PAGE.

Effective Law Enforcement Report Writing

It's more difficult to teach writing and spelling skills than ever before. **Because young people** are questioning the necessity of learning
①
these skills. In the **past decade there have been** a huge increase in audio
②   ③
and video communication devices. This increase has made writing for personal communication **unnecessary**. A person no longer has to write
④
a letter to keep in touch with someone **they know**. A phone call is
⑤
simple, inexpensive, and **needs very little effort**. **They're** few places
⑥   ⑦
in the world where a person can not be reached by phone.

Today, when young people do communicate by **"writing"**, **it's**
⑧
usually by electronic mail on their computers. This form of writing requires little use of formal writing or spelling rules. To make things **simpler** and quick, the old rules are ignored. If you **used** a period,
⑨   ⑩
you don't need to start the next sentence with a capital letter. The phrase "are you" becomes the abbreviated "r u" instead.

Since most people can go through an entire day without being asked to write much more than their name on a credit card **slip, writing** for
⑪
communication may become a thing of the past.

1. (a) Because
    (b) Because of the fact
    (c) Young people
    (d) Since

2. (a) past decade there
    (b) past decade, there
    (c) passed decade there
    (d) passed decades there

GO ON TO THE NEXT PAGE.

3. (a) have been
    (b) has been
    (c) really have been
    (d) really has been

4. (a) unnecessary
    (b) not a necessary
    (c) not a very necessary
    (d) not too necessary

5. (a) they know
    (b) they knew
    (c) he knows
    (d) he knew

6. (a) needs very little effort
    (b) uses very little effort
    (c) takes no effort
    (d) almost effortless

7. (a) They're
    (b) There are
    (c) There are
    (d) They are

8. (a) "writing", it's
    (b) "writing," it's
    (c) "writing," its being done
    (d) "writing", its

9. (a) simpler
    (b) more simple
    (c) most simple
    (d) simple

10. (a) used
    (b) did use
    (c) use
    (d) do use

11. (a) slip, writing
    (b) slip. Writing
    (c) slip; writing
    (d) slip. To write

END OF EXERCISE

1. (c) Young people. *All of the other choices create a sentence fragment rather than a full sentence.*

2. (b) past decade, there. *The word "passed" is the past tense and past participle of the verb "pass." Here, the word "past" is used as an adjective modifying decade. Also, a comma is needed to separate the prepositional phrase, "In the past decade," from the next part of the sentence.*

3. (b) has been. *This covers subject-verb agreement. Since "increase" is singular, the verb must be singular.*

4. (a) unnecessary. *Keep it simple.*

5. (c) he knows. *This covers pronoun agreement. Since person is singular, the verb must be singular. Also, note that (d) improperly changes the tense to past.*

6. (d) almost effortless. *This covers parallel structure. Since "simple" is an adjective and "inexpensive" is an adjective, another adjective must be used—"effortless."*

7. (b) There are. *The other choices present incorrect uses of Their, There, They're and They.*

8. (b) "writing," it's. *This is the correct use of a comma and "it's."*

9. (d) simple. *This item also covers parallel construction. Since the word "simple" is an adjective, another adjective must be used—"quick." Note that "simpler" is a comparative adjective and nothing here is being compare(d)*

10. (c) use. *This is the proper verb tense.*

11. (a) slip, writing. *Choices (b) and (d) are not correct for each one creates a sentence fragment. Choice (c) is an incorrect use of a semi-colon.*

Directions:

The next ten questions continue to test you on your ability to identify errors of standard written English as they appear in sentences. As before, choose the best of the four different versions that follow the passage. If the numbered part of the original sentence meets the requirements of correct and effective English, choose choice (a), which merely repeats the underlined portion. If the bold portion is incorrect, awkward, or ambiguous, select the version that best corrects it and retains the meaning of the original bold phrase.

GO ON TO THE NEXT PAGE.

Effective Law Enforcement Report Writing

Many municipalities across the United States are taking a hard look at educational **requirement's** for police officers. Because policing
①
has changed in recent years and officers must deal with complex

issues. Many cities and towns across the **Country** are requiring an
②   ③
associate's degree, and some **have required** a bachelor's degree.
④

Studies show that officers with college degrees are less likely to abuse their power than **those** who do not have degrees. Also, with the push
⑤
for community policing, officers have to deal with more complex issues and relate to people differently **then** they otherwise would have to do
⑥
during routine police work. An officer on the street today must deal with complex interpersonal issues, myriad legal issues, and

advances in technology.
⑦
Based on a national survey done in 1997, **they're** approximately
⑧
600,000 state and local officers in the nation. Out of those officers, about 32% **has** bachelor's degrees or higher and the number **continue**
⑨   ⑩
to increase 2 percent each year.

1. (a) requirement's
    (b) requirements'
    (c) requirements
    (d) requirement

2. (a) issues. Many
    (b) issues and many
    (c) issues, there are many
    (d) issues, many

GO ON TO THE NEXT PAGE.

3. (a) Country
   (b) country
   (c) countrie
   (d) Countrie

4. (a) have require
   (b) require
   (c) are requiring
   (d) have been required

5. (a) those
   (b) than
   (c) from the way
   (d) since

6. (a) then
   (b) than
   (c) from the way
   (d) since

7. (a) advances in technology
   (b) technology issues
   (c) technology
   (d) new technology

8. (a) they're
   (b) their
   (c) there
   (d) there are

9. (a) has
   (b) has had
   (c) have
   (d) are having

10. (a) continue
    (b) continues
    (c) continuing
    (d) are continuing

END OF EXERCISE

Answers

1. (c) requirements. *Do not use an apostrophe when the word is simply plural and does not show possession.*

2. (d) issues, many. *Choices (a) and (b) create sentence fragments. Choice (c) creates an unclear, run-on sentence.*

3. (b) country. *Choices (c) and (d) contain spelling errors. Choice (a) improperly capitalizes a "common" noun.*

4. (c) are requiring. *This creates a parallel construction.*

5. (a) those. *This is correct.*

6. (b) than. *Choice (a) presents an improper word choice. Choice (c) is not as succinct as (b) Choice (d) makes no sense.*

7. (b) technology issues. *This creates a parallel construction.*

8. (d) there are. *The word presented is the contraction for "They are."*

9. (c) have. *This presents a proper subject-verb agreement. Note that 32% refers to officers.*

10. (b) continues. *This presents a proper subject-verb agreement, "number...continues."*

Proper Spelling is critical for Effective Law Enforcement Reporting. Spelling errors not only detract from the overall quality of a report but also call into question the credibility of the writer.

 For a listing of commonly misspelled words, please refer to the Reference Section of this book beginning on page 281.

Directions:

Each of the following sentences contain a blank line which must be filled with one of the listed answer choices. Read each sentence and select the answer choice that is spelled correctly and properly completes the sentence. Only one answer choice is correct for each problem.

1. The judge made the _____ ℆ _____ that the driver refused to perform the roadside tests because the driver thought he would fail.

   (a) assumsion
   (b) assumption
   (c) ascumssion
   (d) assumtion

2. The _____ b ℆ _____ was intended to identify who lives at 134 Main Street and to determine who was just visiting.

   (a) servalence
   (b) servailance
   (c) surveilance
   (d) surveillance

GO ON TO THE NEXT PAGE.

3. The Supreme Court of the United States recently decided a case, but the ___*A*___ for their decision seemed very confusing.

   (a) rationale
   (b) rashonal
   (c) rashanol
   (d) rational

4. If a patron of the store begins to choke and lose ___*C*___, it is important to call 911 as quickly as possible.

   (a) contousness
   (b) contiousnes
   (c) consciousness
   (d) conscousness

5. Under most circumstances, children should ___*A C*___ be corrected when they act disrespectfully toward an adult.

   (a) imediatley
   (b) immediatly
   (c) immediately
   (d) imediatley

6. I spoke to the kid's father, and he told me that he beat his son upon finding out that he was given a two-day ___*d*___ from school.

   (a) supression
   (b) suspention
   (c) susspension
   (d) suspension

GO ON TO THE NEXT PAGE.

7. The woman was very upset after having ___ C. A ___ a motor vehicle summons in the mail for the accident that she was involved in a week earlier.

   (a) received
   (b) reseaved
   (c) recieved
   (d) receeved

8. When a ___ d ___ chooses to plead not guilty, the court will sometimes provide an attorney for that person.

   (a) defentant
   (b) dephendant
   (c) defendent
   (d) defendant

9. Before you can sell ___ c ___ door-to-door, you must notify the municipal clerk.

   (a) merchandice
   (b) murchindice
   (c) merchandise
   (d) merchendise

10. Do you know the man who recently lost his ___ B ___ because he was caught driving while under the influence of drugs?

   (a) lisence
   (b) license
   (c) liscence
   (d) licence

GO ON TO THE NEXT PAGE.

11. Was the suspect _____ C _____ when he jumped from the car while it was still moving?

(a) intocsicated

(b) entoxcicated

(c) intoxicated

(d) intoxicaded

12. I believe that the driver was slightly ____ A ____ but not incapacitated.

(a) impaired

(b) impared

(c) impeared

(d) imparred

13. The attorney is trying to _____ B _____ the investigation by filing various motions in court.

(a) hindar

(b) hinder

(c) hynder

(d) hindre

14. The most _____ D _____ type of crime fighting involves the use of uniformed patrol officers.

(a) canvansional

(b) convensional

(c) conventionale

(d) conventional

15. If a person gives false information to a police officer, that person may actually be ____ A ____ justice.

(a) obstructing

(b) obstrukting

(c) obstructin

(d) obtructing

GO ON TO THE NEXT PAGE.

16. Some of the commanders really feel strongly about the ___C___ customs in policing.

   (a) treditionale

   (b) traditionile

   (c) traditional

   (d) tredissional

17. The guy in the blue suit likes to _____D_____ confrontations with anyone he can, just to get some attention.

   (a) enstigate

   (b) intricate

   (c) insticate

   (d) instigate

18. When a person makes repeated unwanted telephone calls at very inconvenient hours, it may very well be considered _____A C__.

   (a) harrassment

   (b) harrasment

   (c) harassment

   (d) hirasmant

19. The woman ran out of the building and _____D_____ on the street.

   (a) callappsed

   (b) callapsed

   (c) colapsed

   (d) collapsed

GO ON TO THE NEXT PAGE.

20. When the officer arrived on the scene, the first thing that she saw was the _____*c*_____ woman in the middle of the roadway.

(a) unkontios

(b) uncontious

(c) unconscious

(d) unconcious

21. The new computer system is designed to track missing persons and to help in emergency notifications to all police departments in the event that a _____ occurs.

(a) kidnapping

(b) kidnaping

(c) kinnaping

(d) kiddnapping

22. It is never acceptable to use _____ force as a police officer.

(a) exessive

(b) excesive

(c) eccessive

(d) excessive

23. The very good leads generated from the _____ informant's work led to six new cases.

(a) confidencial

(b) confidential

(c) comfidencial

(d) comfidental

GO ON TO THE NEXT PAGE.

24. The fight against terrorism requires the constant gathering of
_____.

    (a) intelligence

    (b) intelegance

    (c) intelagence

    (d) intellegence

25. The neighbors are all complaining about the _____
traffic on their residential street.

    (a) vehiclar

    (b) vahiculer

    (c) vehicular

    (d) vehiciler

26. The mayor was complaining publicly about the high incidents
of _____ throughout the town.

    (a) larsinee

    (b) larceny

    (c) larsony

    (d) larsonee

27. The roads run _____ to each other, so it does not matter
which road you travel.

    (a) paralel

    (b) parralel

    (c) parallell

    (d) parallel

28. The unlawful burning of a building that belongs to someone
else is commonly called _____.

    (a) arsin

    (b) aerson

    (c) arson

    (d) arhsen

GO ON TO THE NEXT PAGE.

29. For a police officer, maintaining a good _____ is important, so that the proper image is presented to the public.

    (a) apearrence

    (b) appeerance

    (c) appearence

    (d) appearance

30. The patient died after a long fight with _____.

    (a) numonia

    (b) pneumonia

    (c) namonia

    (d) pnuemonea

31. If you want to find out the changes in your payroll deductions, you must check with the _____ department.

    (a) personal

    (b) personnel

    (c) personel

    (d) personnal

32. While _____ on the sidewalk, the boy slipped and fell, sustaining minor injuries.

    (a) traveling

    (b) travelling

    (c) travaling

    (d) travelling

33. The _____ was prosecuted for all of the different offenses he committed.

    (a) tresspasser

    (b) trespassor

    (c) trespasor

    (d) trespasser

GO ON TO THE NEXT PAGE.

34. Crime scene investigation can be a very _____ job.

   (a) teknical

   (b) techniqual

   (c) technical

   (d) techniqal

35. It is hard to understand all of the _____ activity, in which some criminals are involved.

   (a) frawdelant

   (b) fraudlant

   (c) fraudulant

   (d) fraudulent

36. If two people are in a _____ relationship, they are afforded certain protections under the law.

   (a) damestick

   (b) domestick

   (c) domestic

   (d) dimastic

37. The _____ actions of the couple has led to the whole neighborhood being against them.

   (a) illegal

   (b) illigel

   (c) allegal

   (d) illegle

38. Some crimes require that a guilty defendant be _____ for a mandatory minimum sentence.

   (a) encarserated

   (b) incarserated

   (c) encarcerated

   (d) incarcerated

GO ON TO THE NEXT PAGE.

39. Do you know the current location of the _____ offender?

    (a) illedged

    (b) alleged

    (c) aledgeds

    (d) alledged

40. When the legislature passes a new law, it is published as a _____ for the public to read.

    (a) statue

    (b) statued

    (c) statute

    (d) stateud

41. The jury's decision-making process was _____ by the sudden outburst by the defendant's son.

    (a) compromised

    (b) comprimised

    (c) comprimized

    (d) compromized

42. You _____ the jury right from the beginning of the trial.

    (a) prejudgiced

    (b) pregudiced

    (c) prejudiced

    (d) prejudissed

43. The military _____ will not be complete until the early morning hours.

    (a) manuever

    (b) maneuver

    (c) manuevor

    (d) maneuvor

GO ON TO THE NEXT PAGE.

44. Where exactly did the _____ occur last night?

  (a) burglery

  (b) burgarily

  (c) burglary

  (d) burgerily

45. When you arrive at the traffic court, just get in line to talk to the municipal _____.

  (a) prosecutor

  (b) prosecuter

  (c) procurater

  (d) prosicutor

46. The penalties for possession of a _____ usually include jail time.

  (a) weppin

  (b) weapon

  (c) weapan

  (d) weppan

47. If you are calling his _____ into question, you had better have the facts to back it up.

  (a) charactor

  (b) charicter

  (c) chariktor

  (d) character

48. _____ is one of the types of offenses that can really lower the quality of life in a neighborhood.

  (a) Prestotution

  (b) Prostution

  (c) Prostitution

  (d) Prostition

GO ON TO THE NEXT PAGE.

49. The business _____ of a city is the person who controls the business affairs for the municipality.

    (a) administrater

    (b) adminstrator

    (c) administrator

    (d) adminostrater

50. When a death is caused by some type of unlawful action by another, it is commonly referred to as a _____.

    (a) homicide

    (b) homeaside

    (c) homaside

    (d) homacide

GO ON TO THE NEXT PAGE.

Directions:
Each of the following sentences contains a spelling error. Read each sentence and select the answer choice that identifies the word that is spelled incorrectly. Only one answer choice is correct for each problem.

51. Under the laws of this country, a person cannot be discriminated against due to his religeon.

   (a) discriminated

   (b) country

   (c) religeon

   (d) against

52. The generral practice of stopping every car that does not have a valid inspection sticker helps keep our roadways safe.

   (a) generral

   (b) inspection

   (c) roadways

   (d) practice

53. Polititians who betray the public trust should be thrown out of office and sentenced to jail.

   (a) sentenced

   (b) betray

   (c) polititians

   (d) thrown

GO ON TO THE NEXT PAGE.

54. When a benefit is given to an employee, it is nearly impossible to later take it away without causing some type of negetive conflict.

    (a) benefit

    (b) negetive

    (c) impossible

    (d) employee

55. It's worth purchasing a new automobile so the warrentee will cover any expensive repairs that are needed.

    (a) purchasing

    (b) automobile

    (c) expensive

    (d) warrentee

56. Projectiles travelling at a high velocity are likely to penetrate further than the same object at a much lower speed.

    (a) projectiles

    (b) penetrate

    (c) travelling

    (d) velocity

57. Who really understands how the legislature decides what statues to pass and which to deny.

    (a) legislature

    (b) statues

    (c) understands

    (d) decides

GO ON TO THE NEXT PAGE.

58. The nice man was denied the opportunity to coach the youth baseball team because his neighbor once illeged that he harassed her.

(a) opportunity

(b) illeged

(c) harassed

(d) neighbor

59. The weather is really starting to concern me, as the precipatation is starting to convert over from rain to snow rather quickly.

(a) weather

(b) convert

(c) precipatation

(d) concern

60. The prosecutor was disturbed by the false statements that the defense attorney presented to the jury in the closing arguement.

(a) attorney

(b) arguement

(c) disturbed

(d) prosecutor

61. The laws which regulate juvinile behavior are designed to hold offenders accountable for their actions, but also accounts for rehabilitation and redirection.

(a) redirection

(b) accountable

(c) juvinile

(d) behavior

GO ON TO THE NEXT PAGE.

62. Offenders that are under the age of eighteen are adjudicated on the basis of delinqency and are not treated as criminals.

(a) delinqency

(b) adjudicated

(c) eighteen

(d) criminals

63. The confusion of the accident caused the traffic to become conjested and backed up for over three miles.

(a) accident

(b) confusion

(c) conjested

(d) traffic

64. Public discord will often result when the goverment ignores the needs of the people it serves.

(a) discord

(b) public

(c) ignores

(d) goverment

65. The police were called to the exact location of the reported homicide, but only located clothing articles of limited evidental value.

(a) homicide

(b) evidental

(c) reported

(d) limited

GO ON TO THE NEXT PAGE.

66. The nuanses between the two issues are distinct enough that it is not reasonable to think that he could not tell the difference.

    (a) nuanses

    (b) distinct

    (c) reasonable

    (d) difference

67. If you choose to collaborate on the challenging project, you are more likely to experiance success.

    (a) collaborate

    (b) experiance

    (c) challenging

    (d) success

68. Today's society seems to have a problem with allowing for the effective discepline of troubled youths.

    (a) society

    (b) effective

    (c) discepline

    (d) youths

69. An unusual number of people forget that they are required to register their vehicles anually.

    (a) unusual

    (b) register

    (c) vehicles

    (d) anually

GO ON TO THE NEXT PAGE.

70. The awarding of the contract is contingant upon the vendor providing the correct paperwork in a timely manner, while meeting the required contract specifications.

(a) contingant

(b) vendor

(c) timely

(d) specifications

71. The dispatcher needs to comunicate clearly with the officers in the field.

(a) dispatcher

(b) comunicate

(c) clearly

(d) field

72. When dealing with prisoners in a correctional facillity, officers must always be on guard and expect the unexpected.

(a) prisoners

(b) correctional

(c) guard

(d) facillity

73. The fraudulant documents were used to obtain goods and services for which she was not entitled.

(a) fraudulant

(b) document

(c) services

(d) entitled

GO ON TO THE NEXT PAGE.

74. The numerous unbeleivable aspects of the witnesses' version of the events, led to this agency's hesitancy in the filing of any criminal charges.

(a) witnesses'

(b) unbeleivable

(c) hesitancy

(d) version

75. This new statute will supercede our existing policy regarding the use of force.

(a) statute

(b) existing

(c) supercede

(d) regarding

END OF EXERCISE

Answers

1. (b) assumption
2. (d) surveillance
3. (a) rationale
4. (c) consciousness
5. (c) immediately
6. (d) suspension
7. (a) received
8. (d) defendant
9. (c) merchandise
10. (b) license
11. (c) intoxicated
12. (a) impaired
13. (b) hinder
14. (d) conventional
15. (a) obstructing
16. (c) traditional
17. (d) instigate
18. (c) harassment
19. (d) collapsed
20. (c) unconscious
21. (b) kidnaping
22. (d) excessive

23. (b) confidential

24. (a) intelligence

25. (c) vehicular

26. (b) larceny

27. (d) parallel

28. (c) arson

29. (d) appearance

30. (b) pneumonia

31. (b) personnel

32. (a) traveling

33. (d) trespasser

34. (c) technical

35. (d) fraudulent

36. (c) domestic

37. (a) illegal

38. (d) incarcerated

39. (b) alleged

40. (c) statute

41. (a) compromised

42. (c) prejudiced

43. (b) maneuver

44. (c) burglary

45. (a) prosecutor

46. (b) weapon

47. (d) character

48. (c) prostitution

49. (c) administrator

50. (a) homicide

51. (c) religeon (religion)

52. (a) generral (general)

53. (c) polititians (politicians)

54. (b) negetive (negative)

55. (d) warrentee (warrantee)

56. (c) travelling (traveling)

57. (b) statues (statutes)

58. (b) illeged (alleged)

59. (c) precipatation (precipitation)

60.. (b) arguement (argument)

61. (c) juvinile (juvenile)

62. (a) delinqency (delinquency)

63. (c) conjested (congested)

64. (d) goverment (government)

65. (b) evidental (evidential)

66. (a) nuanses (nuances)

67. (b) experiance (experience)

68. (c) discepline (discipline)

69. (d) anually (annually)

70. (a) contingant (contingent)

71. (b) comunicate (communicate)

72. (d) facillity (facilitate)

73. (a) fraudulant (fraudulent)

74. (b) unbeleivable (unbelievable)

75. (c) supercede (supersede) (to replace)

NOTE: Only one word ends in *sede*: *supersede*. Only three words end in *ceed*: *exceed, proceed, succeed*. All other words ending with the sound of "seed" are spelled *cede*: *precede, secede, recede, concede, accede, intercede*.

The competent report writer must have the ability to recognize the proper application of the English language and the grammatical considerations of word usage in written expression.

For a listing of commonly misused words, please refer to the Reference Section of this book beginning on page 269.

Directions:
Each of the following sentences contains a blank which must be completed with the correct selection from the answer choices provided. Read each sentence and select the answer choice which identifies the word or words that most correctly complete the sentence. Only one answer choice is correct for each problem.

1. The dog _____ crossed the street if the owner did not yell so loudly.

    (a) would of

    (b) would have

    (c) wood of

    (d) wood have

2. The people cared deeply about _____ belongings.

    (a) there

    (b) they're

    (c) their

    (d) there's

GO ON TO THE NEXT PAGE.

3. _____ going to be the one to tell the man that his child was in an accident.

   (a) Who

   (b) Whose

   (c) Whose's

   (d) Who's

4. The _____ purse was found down by the shopping mall in a drainage ditch close to the location where she was attacked.

   (a) ladies

   (b) ladys

   (c) ladys'

   (d) lady's

5. After the largest group of protesters leave, the speaker _____ closing down the event.

   (a) begans

   (b) was beginning

   (c) will begin

   (d) has began

6. To succeed, you have to _____ you can accomplish great things.

   (a) belief that

   (b) believe

   (c) be leave

   (d) beliefs

7. The ceiling started to leak _____ the tremendous amount of rain that fell in a one hour period.

   (a) do to

   (b) a cause of

   (c) do from

   (d) due to

GO ON TO THE NEXT PAGE.

8. The man _____ down the street and hopped over a fence to escape.

    (a) run

    (b) runned

    (c) running

    (d) ran

9. Investigator Thomas _____ the detective assigned to the case, until someone else was assigned to take his place.

    (a) is

    (b) was

    (c) will be

    (d) have been

10. Under what circumstances _____ you feel it is okay to lie?

    (a) due

    (b) does

    (c) do

    (d) is

11. Neither Jane _____ Tom should be going anywhere, because they are both grounded.

    (a) nor

    (b) and

    (c) or

    (d) but

12. Brad has a good chance of getting hired because he _____ the test with flying colors.

    (a) past

    (b) pasted

    (c) passed

    (d) pasd

GO ON TO THE NEXT PAGE.

13. When John finally _____ down to fall asleep, the emergency telephone call came in and disrupted everything.

(a) lay

(b) lied

(c) laid

(d) lain

14. If you _____ the same clothing everyday, people will start to think that you don't care about your appearance.

(a) where

(b) ware

(c) were

(d) wear

15. It really _____ matter to me.

(a) don't

(b) doesn't

(c) ain't gonna

(d) wasn't

16. Who _____ that I care what anyone thinks of me?

(a) said

(b) say

(c) sez

(d) sayed

17. The type of cars that you drive _____ to have unnecessary mechanical problems.

(a) seems

(b) seam

(c) seams

(d) seem

GO ON TO THE NEXT PAGE.

18. If the lawnmower's engine _____ , we can cut the grass and make everything look nice.

    (a) operate

    (b) starts

    (c) runned

    (d) ran

19. The microphone _____ work, as long as we can speak loud enough.

    (a) hasn't to

    (b) needs to not

    (c) do not

    (d) does not have to

20. Can you _____ what is being said?

    (a) here

    (b) hear

    (c) hair

    (d) heard

21. The test is just _____ difficult.

    (a) too

    (b) to

    (c) two

    (d) toe

22. The low water level in the nuclear reactor caused the alarms _____ all sound at the same time.

    (a) two

    (b) to

    (c) too

    (d) toe

GO ON TO THE NEXT PAGE.

23. _____ all of the money that we were going to make on this scheme?

(a) Where's

(b) Were's

(c) Wheres'

(d) Wheres

24. You must find _____ own way, if you intend to be happy in life.

(a) you're

(b) you's

(c) your

(d) use

25. If you can't _____ for the light to change to green, then you are impatient.

(a) weight

(b) wate

(c) weit

(d) wait

26. The new recruits were able to _____ the academic record of the last class

(a) accede

(b) exceed

(c) recede

(d) reseed

27. The recent shooting did not _____ Officer Smith.

(a) affect

(b) effect

(c) defect

(d) reflect

GO ON TO THE NEXT PAGE.

28. In our department, we must qualify with our duty weapon _____, that is, twice a year.

  (a) biannually

  (b) semiannually

  (c) both a. and b. are correct.

  (d) neither (a) nor (b) is correct.

29. The drive from the academy was _____ than I expected.

  (a) farther

  (b) further

30. The bias crime was committed on the basis of the victim's _____.

  (a) sex

  (b) gender

31. You have trained Officer Brown _____.

  (a) good

  (b) well

32. If he would _____ listened to me, this never would _____ happened.

  (a) have

  (b) of

  (c) a

33. Which of the below is MOST correct?

  (a) Its amazing how many officers make this mistake

  (b) Its time to go to work

  (c) It's going to take a long time.

  (d) The report's introduction is fine, but its conclusion needs work.

GO ON TO THE NEXT PAGE.

34. Which of the below is NOT correct?

    (a) Today, I will lie in bed.

    (b) Yesterday, I lay in bed

    (c) Many times, I have laid in bed

    (d) Lying in bed is all I do.

35. Which of the below is correct?

    (a) The suspect looks like he is ready to run.

    (b) As with earlier encounters, I treated him with respect.

    (c) We need to recruit another person as you.

    (d) It looks like it is going to rain

36. Which of the below is NOT correct.

    (a) My uniform is cleaner then yours.

    (b) Officer Green finished his tour of duty, then drove home.

    (c) I have more work tonight than you.

    (d) I will finish the work I have, then I will go out with you.

37. Which of the below is correct?

    (a) Whose gun is it?

    (b) Who's the owner of the gun?

    (c) Who's had the most experience?

    (d) Who's experience is best?

38. Recently, the Legislature has written a new _____.

    (a) statue

    (b) statute

GO ON TO THE NEXT PAGE.

39. Officer Young underlined the word to _____ the importance of it.

   (a) accent

   (b) ascent

   (c) assent

40. The sergeant is very _____ at giving orders.

   (a) adapt

   (b) adopt

   (c) adept

   (d) adroit

41. Which _____ do you intend to _____?

   (a) addition, alter

   (b) addition, alter

   (c) edition, altar

   (d) edition, alter

42. The recruits have _____ received their _____.

   (a) all ready, break

   (b) all ready, brake

   (c) already, break

   (d) already, brake

43. The accident victim's _____ was very shallow.

   (a) breath

   (b) breathe

   (c) breadth

GO ON TO THE NEXT PAGE.

44. The investigators planned to _____ the neighborhood for witnesses.

(a) canvas

(b) canvass

(c) cansas

(d) cansass

45. I have received an important _____ from a _____.

(a) correspondents, confidant

(b) correspondents, confident

(c) correspondence, confidant

(d) correspondents, confidant

46. The town _____ met this evening to vote on the measure.

(a) consul

(b) counsel

(c) cownsel

(d) council

47. The officers hated the proposal; there has been growing _____ among the ranks.

(a) decent

(b) dissent

(c) descent

(d) decend

48. The _____ was used to _____ the crowd.

(a) device, disperse

(b) devise, disburse

(c) diverse, disburse

(d) devise, disperse

GO ON TO THE NEXT PAGE.

49. The captain tried to _____ ideas to _____ our options.

    (a) illicit, expend

    (b) elicit, expend

    (c) elicit, expand

    (d) illicit, expand

50. The class was _____ by an _____ speaker.

    (a) felicitated, imminent

    (b) facilitated, eminent

    (c) felicitated, eminent

    (d) facilitated, imminent

51. The police helicopter _____ overhead.

    (a) flu

    (b) flew

    (c) flue

    (d) flued

52. Captain James was _____ a major in the armed forces.

    (a) formally

    (b) formly

    (c) formeraly

    (d) formerly

53. The _____ was located in the airline's _____ .

    (a) gauge, hangar

    (b) gage, hanger

    (c) gauge, hanger

    (d) guage, hangir

GO ON TO THE NEXT PAGE.

54. His argument was _____ irrelevant and inappropriate.

  (a) holly

  (b) holy

  (c) wholly

  (d) holely

55. The training officer's explanation for the _____ of burglaries on the night shift was very _____.

  (a) incidents, inciteful

  (b) incidence, inciteful

  (c) incidents, insightful

  (d) incidence, insightful

56. His approach was very _____, remarkable and _____.

  (a) intense, ingenious

  (b) intents, ingenuous

  (c) intense, disingenuous

  (d) intents, ingenious

57. Unfortunately, Officer Thomas allowed his radar certification to _____.

  (a) elapse

  (b) lapse

  (c) relapse

  (d) elaps

58. The _____ was able to _____ me money for my security deposit.

  (a) lesser, lien

  (b) lessee, lend

  (c) lessor, loan

  (d) lessor, lone

GO ON TO THE NEXT PAGE.

59. The officer is criminally _____ for the assault on the _____.

    (a) liable, marshal

    (b) libel, martial

    (c) liable, marital

    (d) libel, marshal

60. I was able to _____ my stress by telling Officer Sims not to _____ in my personal affairs.

    (a) lesson, metal

    (b) lesson, medal

    (c) lessen, meddle

    (d) lessen, mettle

61. The town council _____ the new _____ today.

    (a) passed, ordinance

    (b) past, ordnance

    (c) passed, ordnance

    (d) past, ordinance

62. The medication for the hospital's _____ was sitting outside on a _____.

    (a) patience, palate

    (b) patients, palette

    (c) pashints, palette

    (d) patients, pallet

63. If you don't hand in your report by 9 this _____, it will be _____.

    (a) mourning, over do

    (b) morning, overdue

    (c) mourning, overdue

    (d) morning, over do

GO ON TO THE NEXT PAGE.

64. The school _____ was able to _____ the interest of the students.

    (a) principle, peak

    (b) principal, peek

    (c) principle, pique

    (d) principal, pique

65. Patrol _____ were able to apprehend the _____ of the crime.

    (a) personnel, perpetrator

    (b) personal, perpetuator

    (c) personnel, perpetuator

    (d) personal, perpetrator

66. During the _____, the district attorney's approach offered a new _____ on the matter.

    (a) prosecution, prospective

    (b) persecution, perspective

    (c) prosecution, perspective

    (d) persecution, prospective

67. Officer White warned the vendor not to _____ his wares too close to the Jones _____.

    (a) pedal, residents

    (b) peddle, residence

    (c) pedal, residence

    (d) peddle, residents

68. When taking this _____ home, you should carefully follow each step listed in the directions _____.

    (a) route, respectively

    (b) root, respectfully

    (c) rout, respectably

    (d) en route, respectably

GO ON TO THE NEXT PAGE.

69. The officers on the day shift _____ that they were required to follow the applicable legal _____.

   (a) recented, precedence

   (b) rezented, precedentz

   (c) resented, precedents

   (d) resented, precedence

70. The new law _____ loitering to sell or buy narcotics on the _____ of the courthouse.

   (a) prescribed, stares

   (b) proscribed, stairs

   (c) proformed, stares

   (d) preformed, stairs

71. We told the informant to be very _____ when he approached the residence and to _____ twice on the door.

   (a) quiet, wrapt

   (b) quite, rapt

   (c) quit, wrap

   (d) quiet, rap

72. Officer Cramer was instructed to _____ one _____ of candy to each of the students.

   (a) proportion, peace

   (b) portion, piece

   (c) apportion, piece

   (d) portion, peace

73. Because the new teacher's approach was _____, all his efforts to teach were in _____.

   (a) specious, vain

   (b) spacious, vein

   (c) specious, vane

   (d) spacious, vain

GO ON TO THE NEXT PAGE.

74. As an established _____ of law enforcement, officers should always be _____.

   (a) tenant, veracious

   (b) tenet, voracious

   (c) tenant, voracious

   (d) tenet, veracious

75. Once the dog picked up _____ scent, he started to _____ them.

   (a) they're, tract

   (b) there, track

   (c) their, track

   (d) they're, track

76. The course required the officers to shoot from a _____ position as _____ in the manual.

   (a) stationery, shone

   (b) stationary, shown

   (c) stationery, shown

   (d) stationary, shone

END OF EXERCISE

Answers

1. (b) would have

2. (c) their (possessive)

3. (d) Who's (Who is)

4. (d) lady's (singular-possessive)

5. (c) will begin (future tense)

6. (b) believe

7. (d) due to

8. (d) ran (past tense)

9. (b) was (past tense)

10. (c) do

11. (a) nor (neither – nor)

12. (c) passed (past tense)

13. (c) laid (past tense)

14. (d) wear

15. (b) doesn't (does not)

16. (a) said (past tense)

17. (d) seem

18. (b) starts (verb – singular)

19. (d) does not have to

20. (b) hear

21. (a) too

22. (b) to

23. (a) Where's (Where is)
24. (c) your (possessive)
25. (d) wait
26. (b) exceed (to surpass)
27. (a) affect (as a verb)
28. (c) both mean twice a year
29. (a) farther (actual distance)
30. (b) gender (social/cultural characteristic)
31. (b) well (as an adverb)
32. (a) have
33. (d) its (possessive); it's (contraction: it is)
34. (c) should be *lain*
35. (b) As with…(used as a conjunction)
36. (a) should be *than* (conjunction)
37. (d) should be *whose* (possessive of who)
38. (b) statute
39. (a) accent (stress in speech or writing)
40. (c) adept (proficient)
41. (d) edition / alter
42. (c) already / break
43. (a) breath (respiration)
44. (b) canvass (to seek, solicit)
45. (c) correspondence / confidant
46. (d) council (legislative body, assembly)
47. (b) dissent (disagreement, disapproval)
48. (a) device / disperse
49. (c) elicit / expand
50. (b) facilitated / eminent
51. (b) flew
52. (d) formerly
53. (a) gauge / hangar
54. (c) wholly (entirely)

55. (d) incidence / insightful

56. (a) intense / ingenious

57. (b) lapse (to become void)

58. (c) lessor (landlord) / loan (to lend)

59. (a) liable / marshal

60. (c) lessen / meddle

61. (a) passed / ordinance

62. (d) patients / pallet

63. (b) morning / overdue

64. (d) principal / pique

65. (a) personnel / perpetrator

66. (c) prosecution / perspective

67. (b) peddle / residence

68. (a) route / respectively

69. (c) resented / precedents

70. (b) proscribed / stairs

71. (d) quiet / rap

72. (c) apportion / piece

73. (a) specious / vain

74. (d) tenet / veracious

75. (c) their / track

76. (b) stationary / shown

Notes

Improper use of punctuation not only detracts from the overall quality of a report, but it can adversely impact on an intended message.

Directions:

Read each sentence and select the answer choice which correctly identifies the punctuation error that exists in the sentence. You will notice that some of the problems include "none" as an answer choice. If you do not feel that an error exists, then choose "none" as your answer. Only one answer choice is correct for each problem.

1. If you can't seem to find it in your heart to care then you should find another job.

   (a) quotations
   (b) comma
   (c) apostrophe
   (d) none

2. That little boys brand new bicycle was stolen from his front yard.

   (a) comma
   (b) colon
   (c) quotations
   (d) apostrophe

GO ON TO THE NEXT PAGE.

3. How do you feel when someone says something critical to you.

(a) quotations

(b) comma

(c) question mark

(d) semicolon

4. The man drove his car too fast and he found that it doesn't pay to speed.

(a) comma

(b) apostrophe

(c) colon

(d) quotations

5. The suspect yelled, I don't think you have the right to arrest me!

(a) comma

(b) quotations

(c) apostrophe

(d) none

6. Just when you started to think that the party was over the music got louder and people started to dance.

(a) quotations

(b) comma

(c) question mark

(d) colon

7. Who is knocking at the back door?

(a) quotations

(b) comma

(c) question mark

(d) none

GO ON TO THE NEXT PAGE.

8. The students' belongings were left in the classrooms during the fire drill.

(a) quotations

(b) comma

(c) apostrophe

(d) none

9. My neighbor Mary Marshall said that she might be able to help us this weekend.

(a) apostrophe

(b) commas

(c) question mark

(d) semicolon

10. Whats the problem with Tony?

(a) quotations

(b) comma

(c) question mark

(d) apostrophe

11. I went to the store yesterday and found that it simply was not worth the hassle of fighting through the crowds for the sales.

(a) quotations

(b) comma

(c) apostrophe

(d) none

12. The use of this agencies police vehicles is limited to sworn personnel only.

(a) quotations

(b) comma

(c) apostrophe

(d) hyphen

GO ON TO THE NEXT PAGE.

13. Jason should've gone to the bank before he tried to go shopping for new clothes.

(a) comma

(b) apostrophe

(c) period

(d) none

14. My favorite part of the song comes in the third verse when the performer sings, I don't want you back.

(a) quotations

(b) comma

(c) question mark

(d) apostrophe

15. What kind of person sells their child to total strangers on the open market for a profit.

(a) quotations

(b) comma

(c) question mark

(d) apostrophe

16. The crowd gathered around the man and began to physically assault him in direct view of three police officers.

(a) quotations

(b) comma

(c) apostrophe

(d) none

17. Marks house was one of the four homes that burned to the ground in that large fire last week.

(a) quotations

(b) comma

(c) question mark

(d) apostrophe

GO ON TO THE NEXT PAGE.

18. Under the circumstances I think the best approach is to just ignore the conflict and move forward.

(a) quotations

(b) comma

(c) question mark

(d) apostrophe

19. The author John Jones wrote the book for people who have experienced traumatic events in their lives.

(a) quotations

(b) commas

(c) question mark

(d) apostrophe

20. How do people find it so easy to just look the other way.

(a) quotations

(b) comma

(c) question mark

(d) none

21. The womans bathroom was completely destroyed after her husband forgot to shut the water off.

(a) quotations

(b) comma

(c) apostrophe

(d) none

22. The Attorney General publishes guidelines which all police officers must adhere to in the performance of their duties.

(a) quotations

(b) comma

(c) apostrophe

(d) none

GO ON TO THE NEXT PAGE.

23. When a new law is passed by the legislature and signed by the governor it is important that every police agency inform the officers exactly what the law entails.

 (a) quotations

 (b) comma

 (c) apostrophe

 (d) none

24. It really doesn't matter what other people think about Johns car.

 (a) quotations

 (b) comma

 (c) question mark

 (d) apostrophe

25. Its fun to watch a dog chase its tail.

 (a) quotations

 (b) comma

 (c) apostrophe

 (d) none

26. If you really think that you are right then you should file an appeal.

 (a) quotations

 (b) comma

 (c) question mark

 (d) apostrophe

27. Having been a student for the past six years, I think that I've earned the right to criticize the policies of the school.

 (a) apostrophe

 (b) comma

 (c) question mark

 (d) none

GO ON TO THE NEXT PAGE.

28. Under the new guidelines an officer is required to report the use of force that rises above the level of just mere physical contact.

    (a) quotations

    (b) comma

    (c) apostrophe

    (d) none

29. Chief Martin did tell us that the stations radio console needs to be replaced.

    (a) quotations

    (b) comma

    (c) apostrophe

    (d) none

30. When I was asked if I wanted the job, I replied honestly by saying, I don't know.

    (a) quotations

    (b) comma

    (c) apostrophe

    (d) none

END OF EXERCISE

1. (b) comma - If you can't seem to find it in your heart to care, then you should find another job.

2. (d) apostrophe - That little boy's brand new bicycle was stolen from his front yard.

3. (c) question mark - How do you feel when someone says something critical to you?

4. (a) comma - The man drove his car too fast, and he found that it doesn't pay to speed.

5. (b) quotations - The suspect yelled, "I don't think you have the right to arrest me!"

6. (b) comma - Just when you started to think that the party was over, the music got louder and people started to dance.

7. (d) none

8. (d) none

9. (b) commas - My neighbor, Mary Marshall, said that she might be able to help us this weekend.

10. (d) apostrophe - What's the problem with Tony?

11. (d) none

12. (c) apostrophe - The use of this agency's police vehicles is limited to sworn personnel only.

13. (d) none

14. (a) quotations - My favorite part of the song comes in the third verse when the performer sings, "I don't want you back."

15. (c) question mark - What kind of person sells their child to total strangers on the open market for a profit?

16. (d) none

17. (d) apostrophe - Mark's house was one of the four homes that burned to the ground in that large fire last week.

18. (b) comma - Under the circumstances, I think the best approach is to just ignore the conflict and move forward.

19. (b) commas - The author, John Jones, wrote the book for people who have experienced traumatic events in their lives.

20. (c) question mark - How do people find it so easy to just look the other way?

21. (c) apostrophe - The woman's bathroom was completely destroyed after her husband forgot to shut the water off.

22. (d) none

23. (b) comma - When a new law is passed by the legislature and signed by the governor, it is important that every police agency inform the officers exactly what the law entails.

24. (d) apostrophe - It really doesn't matter what other people think about John's car.

25. (c) apostrophe - It's fun to watch a dog chase its tail.

26. (b) comma - If you really think that you are right, then you should file an appeal.

27. (d) none

28. (b) comma - Under the new guidelines, an officer is required to report the use of force that rises above the level of just mere physical contact.

29. (c) apostrophe - Chief Martin did tell us that the station's radio console needs to be replaced.

30. (a) quotations - When I was asked if I wanted the job, I replied honestly by saying, "I don't know."

The following exercise, consisting of one fact pattern and ten short-answer questions, is designed to sharpen reading comprehension skills.

Directions:
First, preview the questions, next read the report, then answer the questions.

GO ON TO THE NEXT PAGE.

THE INTRUDER

At 1:45 p.m., August 31, 2001, I was advised to contact the Smiths' home on Route 37, one mile south of Toms River, New Jersey, to investigate an attempted burglary. At 2:15 p.m., August 31, 2001, Susan Smith, age 43, of Route 37, was contacted at her home. She said that yesterday, at about 12:45 p.m., a white and blue vehicle, occupied by two men, stopped in front of her home. A young man, about 20 years old, with sandy, bushy hair, came to the front door and knocked. Mrs. Smith would not go to the door since she did not know the person, and after a few minutes he returned to the white older-model car, and drove south on Route 37.

About ten minutes later, the car returned, let the young man out, drove south on Route 37, and parked in a side road about one-quarter mile south of the Smith's home. Mrs. Smith saw the man walking along the driveway on the north side of her house, but she thought that he was going to the woods behind the house. At the time, Mrs. Smith was working in the home's rear office with her associate, Mary Sutley. A few minutes later, she heard a noise in her kitchen and looked in to see the young man walking into the front room. He had apparently entered the house through the unlocked side door. Mrs. Smith stepped into the kitchen and asked the young man what he was doing. Mrs. Smith startled the young man, causing him to drop the plate he was holding, and run through the house, out the front door and into the woods east of the house, where he snagged and ripped his pant leg on a jagged tree stump. At this time, the vehicle that the young man had arrived in was still parked just south of the house, and it remained there for about five minutes after the subject ran from the house.

During this time, Mrs. Smith loaded a rifle, then got a paper and pencil to write down the license plate number of the car. Mary suggested calling the police. When the car passed the house northbound, Mrs. Smith copied the license plate number of the Chevy as 263ADRG, but she was unsure of the first three digits. She thought, perhaps, that the license plate displayed on the car was a Florida plate. Nothing was taken from the house by the young man, and neither Mrs. Smith nor Mary was harmed. Mrs. Smith ultimately decided to follow Mary's suggestion.

GO ON TO THE NEXT PAGE.

THE INTRUDER

1. Who called the police?

    _____

    _____

2. Who is (are) the victim(s)?

    _____

    _____

3. Are there any witnesses?

    _____

    _____

4. What description of the vehicle was given?

    _____

    _____

5. What physical evidence was left?

    _____

    _____

6. What action was taken by the police?

    _____

    _____

7. What crime(s) was (were) committed?

    _____

    _____

8. When was (were) the crime(s) committed?

    _____

    _____

9. When was (were) the crime(s) reported?

    _____

    _____

10. How was (were) the crime(s) discovered?

    _____

    _____

END OF EXERCISE

1. Mrs. Smith

2. Susan Smith

3. Susan Smith. Mary Sutley did not see the intruder. Note, however, that she could be considered a witness to other events, such as the time of the incident and Susan's actions.

4. A white and blue, older model Chevy, possible Florida registration, 263 ADRG.

5. Possible fingerprints on plate, and, possibly, part of a pant leg left on the jagged tree stump.

6. Contacted Mrs. Smith. It is unclear from the facts whether the officer documented the report in writing.

7. Burglary, criminal attempt theft, criminal mischief.

8. August 30, 2001, at 1:00 p.m.

9. Sometime prior to 1:45 p.m. on August 31, 2001.

10. Mrs. Smith confronted the intruder in her home.

The following exercise is designed to sharpen reading comprehension skills.

Directions:

Questions 1 through 15 are based on the following Policy on Sexual Harassment in the Workplace. Answers should be based on this policy alone and not on any State, County or local policy nor on any particular State law or procedure. Read each of the simulated situations which follow the Policy and, after a careful review of the Policy, determine whether (a) The employee's conduct violates the policy and/or procedures; (b) The employee's conduct does not violate the policy and/or procedures; (c) The policy and/or procedures do not apply; or (d) The facts presented are insufficient to make a determination.

GO ON TO THE NEXT PAGE.

POLICY

Sexual Harassment in the Workplace

I. POLICY

A. It is the policy of this Department to provide a work environment that is free from discriminatory practices. In recognition of the personal dignity and worth of each person employed by, or professionally associated with, this Department, this policy outlawing sexual harassment in the workplace is hereby adopted. It is designed to foster a work environment free of sexual harassment, and to establish procedures for dealing with sexual harassment when it occurs.

B. All employees, female or male, have a right to a work environment free from all forms of unlawful discrimination and conduct which can be considered harassing, coercive or disruptive, including sexual harassment. Sexual harassment is a form of employee misconduct which undermines the integrity of the employment relationship. Sexual harassment debilitates morale and interferes with work productivity and, therefore, will not be tolerated. Any employee who engages in sexual harassment is subject to discipline, up to and including dismissal.

C. This policy applies to all employees of this Department, both sworn and civilian.

II. DEFINITIONS

A. No form of sexual harassment, as defined hereafter, shall be tolerated by this Department. Sexual harassment is defined as unwelcome sexual advances, requests for sexual favors and other verbal or physical conduct based on gender when:

1. Submission to such conduct is made either explicitly or implicitly a term or condition of an individual's employment;

GO ON TO THE NEXT PAGE.

2. Submission to or rejection of such conduct by an individual is used as the basis for employment decisions affecting such individual (such as recommendations for promotion or retention; transfer; duty assignments; vehicle assignments; meal breaks; early dismissal; etc.); or

3. Such conduct has the purpose or effect of unreasonably interfering with an individual's work performance or creating an intimidating, hostile or offensive working environment including, but not limited to:

    a. physical assaults of a sexual nature, such as sexual assault or criminal sexual contact, or the attempt to commit these offenses;

    b. intentional physical conduct which is sexual in nature, such as touching, pinching, patting, grabbing, brushing against another employee's body, or poking another employee's body;

    c. unwanted sexual advances, propositions, sexual flirtations, or other unwelcome sexual comments, such as

        (1) sexually oriented gestures, noises, remarks, jokes, or comments about a person's sexuality or sexual experience directed at or made in the presence of any employee who indicates or has indicated in any way that such conduct in his or her presence is unwelcome; or

        (2) preferential treatment or promise of preferential treatment to an employee for submitting to sexual conduct, including soliciting or attempting to solicit any employee to engage in sexual activity for compensation or reward; or

        (3) subjecting, or threatening to subject, an employee to unwelcome sexual attention or conduct; or

        (4) intentionally making performance of the employee's job more difficult because of the employee's sex.

GO ON TO THE NEXT PAGE.

     d.   showing or displaying pornographic or sexually explicit or discriminatory objects, pictures, publications or displays anywhere in the workplace, or at a work-related function, such as

        (1) displaying, or otherwise publicizing in the work environment, pictures, posters, calendars, graffiti, objects, promotional materials, reading materials, or other materials that are sexually revealing, sexually suggestive, sexually demeaning, or pornographic; or

        (2) displaying signs or other materials purporting to segregate an employee by sex in any area of the workplace, other than restrooms and similar semi-private locker/changing rooms.

     e.   retaliation for sexual harassment complaints, such as

        (1) disciplining, changing work assignments of, providing inaccurate work information to, or refusing to cooperate or discuss work-related matters with any employee because that employee has complained about or resisted harassment, discrimination or retaliation; or

        (2) intentionally pressuring another person to give false information about an alleged incident of sexual harassment for the purpose of covering up such incident.

B. Conduct under Section B., above, by a supervisor, other superior or by co-workers constitutes prohibited sexual harassment when a reasonable person of the same sex in the employee's position would consider it sufficiently severe or pervasive to alter the conditions of employment or to create an intimidating, hostile or offensive working environment.

GO ON TO THE NEXT PAGE.

III. REPORTING AND INVESTIGATING SEXUAL HARASSMENT

A. Employees

1. Employees subjected to sexual harassment are encouraged, whether directly or through a third party, to notify the alleged harasser that the behavior in question is offensive and unwelcome. However, failure to do so does not preclude filing a complaint.

2. Any employee who believes that he/she or another employee has been the subject of sexual or other prohibited harassment or discrimination should promptly report the matter to his or her immediate supervisor, a higher level administrator, any member of the Department's management, or Internal Affairs.

3. Employees are required to report any instance of sexual or other prohibited harassment or discrimination immediately. This will enable the Department to investigate and resolve the matter promptly and effectively.

B. Supervisors and Managers

1. In order to ensure the integrity of the work environment, supervisory and managerial personnel are required to ensure strict adherence to, and compliance with, this policy.

2. Upon becoming informed of, or becoming aware of possible sexual harassment, managers/supervisors shall:

   a. Take appropriate immediate action to stop the harassing behavior;

   b. Assure the complainant that the matter will be handled in a proactive, discreet and confidential manner;

   c. Inform the employee of his/her right to file a discrimination complaint; and

   d. Notify the Internal Affairs Unit of the incident and the action taken.

GO ON TO THE NEXT PAGE.

227

C. The Complaint Reporting Process. There are various ways in which employees may file sexual harassment or discrimination complaints within or outside the agency, either concurrently or sequentially. Complaints may be filed with:

1. The Internal Affairs Unit/Officer;

2. The employee's direct supervisor;

3. Other supervisors/managers in the employee's chain of command;

4. Officials outside the employee's chain of command

   a. The complainant may initiate a sexual harassment or other discrimination complaint outside the employee's direct chain of command, up to the chief executive officer, if filing the complaint using the normal chain of command or the Internal Affairs Unit would pose a conflict of interest by virtue of the alleged harasser having any involvement in the intake, investigative or decision-making process.

   b. The complainant may also initiate a sexual harassment or other discrimination complaint directly with the State Division on Civil Rights or the United States Equal Employment Opportunity and Affirmative Action Commission, if filing the complaint with a member of the Department would pose a conflict of interest by virtue of the alleged harasser having any involvement in the intake, investigative or decision-making process.

   c. Other forums may include the State Superior Court and the Federal District Court.

D. Investigation/Confidentiality

1. All complaints will be addressed promptly and investigated thoroughly.

2. All parties to the complaint shall be afforded all of the protection provided in confidential department internal affairs investigations.

GO ON TO THE NEXT PAGE.

3. At the conclusion of the investigation, the Department will take appropriate remedial action. Any employee who is found to have committed an act of sexual harassment will be subject to disciplinary action up to and including termination. False accusations of sexual harassment will result in disciplinary action up to and including termination.

4. Protection of All Parties

   a. All complaints will be addressed promptly and investigated thoroughly, and all parties to the complaint shall be afforded all of the protection provided in confidential internal investigations.

   b. In no case will the complaining employee be required to confront the alleged harasser face to face, nor to discuss the allegations in the presence of the harasser.

   c. To the extent possible, the sexual harassment investigative proceedings will be conducted in a manner which protects the confidentiality of the complainant, the alleged harasser and all witnesses.

E. Prohibition Against Retaliation

   1. It shall be a violation of this policy for any employee to retaliate against a victim, complainant, or witness for such party's involvement or assistance in a sexual or other prohibited harassment investigation or complaint.

   2. Threats, intimidation, coercion, or any other form of retaliation against the complainant or any other party based on involvement in the complaint process shall be cause for disciplinary action.

GO ON TO THE NEXT PAGE.

F. Remedial Action for employees found in violation of this policy may be progressive in nature and include:

1. Referral to counseling

2. Oral Reprimand

3. Written Reprimand

4. Reassignment

5. Suspension

6. Demotion

7. Termination

8. Criminal prosecution

This Department is committed to maintaining a heightened awareness of the personal dignity of others by fostering a work environment that is free of sexual and other forms of unlawful harassment and discrimination.

GO ON TO THE NEXT PAGE.

Simulated Situations
Policy on Sexual Harassment in the Workplace

1. Bill Hartman, a Coast News employee, delivers newspapers to the police department each morning. Every day, after dropping off the papers, Bill pats the secretary on the buttocks and says, "See ya, toots."

   (a) The employee's conduct violates the policy and/or procedures.

   (b) The employee's conduct does not violate the policy and/or procedures.

   (c) The policy and/or procedures do not apply.

   (d) The facts presented are insufficient to make a determination.

2. Tom, a captain in the investigative section, calls a staff meeting and asks Mary, the only female detective at the meeting, to take notes, make copies of a memo for everyone, and get coffee for everyone.

   (a) The employee's conduct violates the policy and/or procedures.

   (b) The employee's conduct does not violate the policy and/or procedures.

   (c) The policy and/or procedures do not apply.

   (d) The facts presented are insufficient to make a determination.

3. Bob, a police lieutenant, asked Cathy, a new police officer, to go out with him on three occasions. After she refused, Bob moved her from patrol duties to the less prestigious and less challenging job of working in the dispatch room.

   (a) The employee's conduct violates the policy and/or procedures.

   (b) The employee's conduct does not violate the policy and/or procedures.

   (c) The policy and/or procedures do not apply.

   (d) The facts presented are insufficient to make a determination.

GO ON TO THE NEXT PAGE.

4. Jim, the department's janitor, continually makes comments to Sara, the department's matron, such as, "You look dynamite in those tight jeans." The comments make Sara uncomfortable.

    (a) The employee's conduct violates the policy and/or procedures.

    (b) The employee's conduct does not violate the policy and/or procedures.

    (c) The policy and/or procedures do not apply.

    (d) The facts presented are insufficient to make a determination.

5. Trent works in the records section of the department. At his work station, he put a picture of a woman in a bikini up on the wall. Harriet, who also works in the records section, found this amusing and hung a picture of a man in jockey shorts next to the woman in the bikini.

    (a) The employees' conduct violates the policy and/or procedures.

    (b) The employees' conduct does not violate the policy and/or procedures.

    (c) The policy and/or procedures do not apply.

    (d) The facts presented are insufficient to make a determination.

6. After new police officers are hired and sworn in, they must attend the police academy. Carol Ann, a new police trainee at the academy, told her friend, "The male trainees are always telling dirty jokes and looking at me. This bothers me so much, I can't concentrate on my studies."

    (a) The employees' conduct violates the policy and/or procedures.

    (b) The employees' conduct does not violate the policy and/or procedures.

    (c) The policy and/or procedures do not apply.

    (d) The facts presented are insufficient to make a determination.

GO ON TO THE NEXT PAGE.

7. Officer Samantha Smith approached Captain James and advised him that her sergeant, Bill Loyd, has been making what she believed to be inappropriate comments of a sexual nature. Smith states that Sergeant Loyd always waits for the other officers on her squad to leave the squad room before he makes the comments. Smith did not approach the lieutenant because the lieutenant and Sergeant Loyd are very good friends. Captain James immediately advises Smith that she has violated the chain of command and must first register her complaint with the lieutenant.

    (a) The captain's conduct violates the policy and/or procedures.

    (b) The captain's conduct does not violate the policy and/or procedures.

    (c) The policy and/or procedures do not apply.

    (d) The facts presented are insufficient to make a determination.

8. Sergeant Traymore tells Dispatcher Colleen Jones that she dresses nicely and that he likes her taste in sweaters.

    (a) The employee's conduct violates the policy and/or procedures.

    (b) The employee's conduct does not violate the policy and/or procedures.

    (c) The policy and/or procedures do not apply.

    (d) The facts presented are insufficient to make a determination.

9. Barbara has always been considered "one of the guys." She has always held her own with the jokes, even the sexual ones; and with regard to the pranks, dished out as much as she took. Yesterday, however, she told her supervisor, "The guys are making crude comments and jokes all the time. They're not funny to me and I can't stand it any longer."

    (a) The employees' conduct violates the policy and/or procedures.

    (b) The employees' conduct does not violate the policy and/or procedures.

    (c) The policy and/or procedures do not apply.

    (d) The facts presented are insufficient to make a determination.

GO ON TO THE NEXT PAGE.

10. Deputy Chief Kathy Corris met with Lieutenant Candy, one of the candidates for police captain, to discuss a number of matters, including performance. During the conversation, she praised the work Candy had done over the years and commented that she hoped the professional performance would continue now that he is up for promotion to captain. Lieutenant Candy stated that he would be willing to do whatever was necessary to get promoted, even if it was personal.

    (a) The employee's conduct violates the policy and/or procedures.

    (b) The employee's conduct does not violate the policy and/or procedures.

    (c) The policy and/or procedures do not apply.

    (d) The facts presented are insufficient to make a determination.

11. Iris Spears is a new clerk for the commander of the narcotics unit. Her duties require her to interact with all the members of the unit. On hot summer days, she wears flimsy, revealing dresses without a slip, or extremely tight-fitting jeans or slacks. She never wears a bra. In her conversations with the detectives in the office, she makes frequent remarks with double meanings. For example, she once asked Detective Harper to move a filing cabinet, and remarked, "I didn't realize you were so strong. Do you have other things that are as strong as your arms?"

    (a) The employee's conduct violates the policy and/or procedures.

    (b) The employee's conduct does not violate the policy and/or procedures.

    (c) The policy and/or procedures do not apply.

    (d) The facts presented are insufficient to make a determination.

GO ON TO THE NEXT PAGE.

12. Lieutenant Proder always calls every woman in his office "Babe" or "Honey." He refers to his wife this way, as well as his secretary. When women attend staff meetings or briefings, he also addresses them as "Babe" or "Honey." He is a very friendly, down-to-earth person and will often put his arm around a woman's shoulder when he is talking to her.

(a) The employee's conduct violates the policy and/or procedures.

(b) The employee's conduct does not violate the policy and/or procedures.

(c) The policy and/or procedures do not apply.

(d) The facts presented are insufficient to make a determination.

13. Officers Cohen and Ramos have an ongoing rivalry and try to outdo each other every chance they get. Today, they each went out of their way to help a female co-worker get oriented to some new patrol equipment. This "good natured" competition turned into an all-out fist fight.

(a) The employees' conduct violates the policy and/or procedures.

(b) The employees' conduct does not violate the policy and/or procedures.

(c) The policy and/or procedures do not apply.

(d) The facts presented are insufficient to make a determination.

GO ON TO THE NEXT PAGE.

14. Chief Tea has just recently learned of the commission of sexual harassment by Lieutenant Prabosko. The Chief approached the victim, Officer Buffy, and asked if she wished to speak to him about the lieutenant's behavior. Officer Buffy explained that, over the past several months, the lieutenant has been making rude sexual comments to her, and demanding sexual favors. She also explained that on one occasion, the lieutenant walked into the female officers' locker room when only she was present, grabbed his crotch, and said, "This is what you got to take care of if you want to make it on this department." After listening to the facts, Chief Tea told Officer Buffy that he would take appropriate immediate action to stop the harassing behavior. He assured her that the matter would be handled in a proactive, discreet and confidential manner; and also informed her that she did not have to take any further action because he would handle the matter personally.

    (a) The Chief's conduct violates the policy and/or procedures.

    (b) The Chief's conduct does not violate the policy and/or procedures.

    (c) The policy and/or procedures do not apply.

    (d) The facts presented are insufficient to make a determination.

15. Sam is homosexual and works on the bicycle squad with Lenny. Sam has asked Lenny out several times, and Lenny has refused. Because Lenny refuses to go out with him, Sam begins to joke around with him, calling him a homosexual. Lenny gets upset and very uncomfortable.

    (a) The employee's conduct violates the policy and/or procedures.

    (b) The employee's conduct does not violate the policy and/or procedures.

    (c) The policy and/or procedures do not apply.

    (d) The facts presented are insufficient to make a determination.

END OF EXERCISE

1. (c) *The policy and/or procedures do not apply.* Bill is not an "employee" of the police department. *See* Section I.C.

2. (d) *The facts presented are insufficient to make a determination.* If, in asking Mary to perform such tasks, the captain selected her because of her gender, and her submission to such requests was expressly or impliedly used as a basis for future employment decisions, the captain's conduct may constitute sexual discrimination and may also violate the policy.

3. (a) *The employee's conduct violates the policy and/or procedures.* This is *quid pro quo* sexual harassment. *See* Section II.A.2.

4. (a) *The employee's conduct violates the policy and/or procedures.* This is "hostile work environment" sexual harassment. *See* Section II.A.3.

5. (d) *The facts presented are insufficient to make a determination.* If the actions of Trent and Harriet create an offensive working environment for others in the workplace, the conduct would violate the policy. *See* Section II.A.3.d.

6. (a) *The employee's conduct violates the policy and/or procedures.* This is "hostile work environment" sexual harassment. *See* Section II.A.3.

7. (a) *The captain's conduct violates the policy and/or procedures.* Under the policy, Officer Smith is not required to adhere to the strict chain of command. Section III.A.2. permits reporting of the matter to "any member of the Department's management." *See also* Section III.C.4.

8. (b) *The employee's conduct does not violate the policy and/or procedures.* Note, however, that if the comment was made in an offensive and sexual tone, the opposite conclusion should be reached.

9. (a) *The employees' conduct violates the policy and/or procedures.* This is "hostile work environment" sexual harassment. *See* Section II.A.3.

10. (d) *The facts presented are insufficient to make a determination.* While Candy's statements may not be considered "sexual harassment," it is a form of enticement. If the enticement is of a sexual nature, and if Corris accepts an offer of sexual services in exchange for the promotion, she would be in violation of Section II.A.2 of the policy (*quid pro quo* sexual harassment).

11. (b) *The employee's conduct does not violate the policy and/or procedures.* While Iris' behavior is certainly inappropriate, it is not sexually harassing under the policy. She should be counseled about her dress and inappropriate behavior.

12. (b) *The employee's conduct does not violate the policy and/or procedures.* This is a close call. While the lieutenant's behavior is not necessarily sexually harassing, it is nonetheless inappropriate work behavior. If his behavior graduates into targeting a specific person or creating a hostile environment, it could become violative of the policy.

13. (b) *The employee's conduct does not violate the policy and/or procedures.* While the actions of Officers Cohen and Ramos may constitute improper behavior, their actions do not constitute sexual harassment within the meaning of the policy.

14. (a) *The Chief's conduct violates the policy and/or procedures.* Under Section III.B.2, upon becoming informed of, or becoming aware of possible sexual harassment, the chief was required to: (a) Take appropriate immediate action to stop the harassing behavior; b. Ensure the complainant that the matter will be handled in a proactive, discreet and confidential manner; (c) Inform the employee of her right to file a discrimination complaint; and (d) Notify the Internal Affairs Unit of the incident and the action taken.

15. (a) *The employee's conduct violates the policy and/or procedures.* This is "hostile work environment" sexual harassment. *See* Section II.A.3.

COHERENT WRITING
PARAGRAPH STRUCTURE

A paragraph is a series of sentences that develop one topic. Generally, the first sentence in the paragraph sets forth the main topic or subject of the paragraph. The sentences that follow this "topic sentence" should be closely related to it, and should proceed in a logical, coherent order. The information in a paragraph may be developed in several ways. For example, the information may be developed in chronological order, in order of importance, from the general to the specific, as a comparison or contrast, or as a cause and effect. Sentence arrangement may also proceed by first setting forth the topic sentence, and then adding supporting reasons, facts or examples.

Here are a few tips for creating logical coherent paragraphs: Pay particular attention to (1) pronouns which may refer back to a previously written sentence; (2) words showing order, such as "first," "second," "third," "last"; (3) words showing spatial relationships, such as "above," "below," "over," "under," "around," "besides"; (4) words that add information, such as "also," "in addition," "moreover," "furthermore," "again"; (5) words that show cause, effect or conclusion, such as "because," "therefore," "inasmuch as," "accordingly," "as a result," "consequently"; and (6) words that show contrast or restriction, such as "since," "yet," "although," "otherwise."

Directions:

The following sentences are listed out of order. Read all of the sentences and choose the BEST order in which to arrange the sentences so that they create a succinct, logical and comprehensible paragraph. In all cases, you should attempt to locate the "topic" sentence, which is usually the first sentence in the paragraph, and then locate those sentences that support the topic sentence in a logical progression of information. The last sentence usually presents a statement representing a conclusion to the thought/information presented in the paragraph.

GO ON TO THE NEXT PAGE.

1. Arrange the following sentences in proper order to create a coherent, well-written paragraph.

(1) He then started the car by "hot wiring" the ignition.

(2) Johnson drove off at a high rate of speed.

(3) At 3:00 p.m., Mike Johnson broke into a green, two-door Ford.

(4) Officer Jones witnessed the entire event and closely followed Johnson.

    (a) 1-2-3-4

    (b) 3-1-2-4

    (c) 4-3-1-2

    (d) 3-4-1-2

2. Arrange the following sentences in proper order to create a coherent, well-written paragraph.

(1) Instead, they become overly involved in controlling the routine activities of their subordinates and, even worse, they do the actual work themselves, often under the mistaken belief that they will win the favor of their subordinates.

(2) Over-supervision is the most common error made by new supervisors.

(3) However, most workers resent such an approach and often view it as indicative of a lack of confidence in their abilities.

(4) In their zeal to get the job done, they forget that their new position requires them to delegate authority to their subordinates.

(5) To complicate the matter even more, over-supervision also curtails worker initiative, creates morale problems and decreases respect for the supervisor.

    (a) 4-1-2-3-5

    (b) 2-4-1-3-5

    (c) 2-5-4-3-1

    (d) 4-3-2-1-5

GO ON TO THE NEXT PAGE.

3. Arrange the following sentences in proper order to create a coherent, well-written paragraph.

(1) Very few officers have the ability to recall from memory all the details of a complex case or incident several hours, days or months later, when it becomes necessary to prepare a formal report or testify in court.

(2) In this respect, the notes you record in your field notebook may be considered an "index" to your memory.

(3) Above all else, the notes you record in your field notebook should be accurate, clear and concise.

(4) With practice, you will develop a form of shorthand that will assist you in quickly recording the relevant details of an event without the need to overload pages with unnecessary words.

(5) While there is no need to record every single detail about an incident in your field notebook, you should record enough detail about the incident to refresh your memory of related facts.

    (a) 5-4-3-2-1

    (b) 4-5-1-3-2

    (c) 1-5-2-4-3

    (d) 1-5-3-4-2

4. Arrange the following sentences in proper order to create a coherent, well-written paragraph.

(1) This is dead wrong.

(2) As a demonstrative form of evidence, the crime-scene sketch provides a graphic display of the scene (in whole or in part) with accurate measurements of distances between objects.

(3) Many officers fall into the trap of believing that sketches are not necessary when the crime scene is being processed and photographed by crime-scene personnel.

    (a) 1-2-3

    (b) 3-2-1

    (c) 2-1-3

    (d) 3-1-2

GO ON TO THE NEXT PAGE.

5. Arrange the following sentences in proper order to create a coherent, well-written paragraph.

(1) Another is the "Investigation" or "Supplementary Investigation Report."

(2) The hallmark of the competent law enforcement officer is the ability to record his or her observations in a clear, concise and readily understandable manner.

(3) These are the official documents which provide the spark which fires the other components of the criminal justice system into action.

(4) One of the means through which an officer's observations and actions are recorded is the "Incident" or "Operations Report."

    (a) 1-2-3-4

    (b) 4-3-2-1

    (c) 2-4-1-3

    (d) 2-3-1-4

6. Arrange the following sentences in proper order to create a succinct, well-written paragraph.

(1) On July 3, 2001, at 12:20 p.m., I, Officer Brent Young, was dispatched to 123 Main Street in reference to a call of a "man down and bleeding."

(2) At the time, Samson was bleeding from his forehead.

(3) Upon my arrival at 123 Main Street, I was met by the building superintendent, Lonny Anderson.

(4) He stated that he wasn't watching where he was walking and tripped down the stairs.

(5) He stated that while he was eating lunch, he heard a loud thud in the hallway of the building.

(6) He then immediately looked out his door and saw his neighbor, Gregg Samson, lying on the floor.

(7) I approached Samson and asked what had happened.

(8) The building at 123 Main Street is a three-story apartment building.

    (a) 1-8-3-5-6-2-7-4

    (b) 1-2-3-4-8-7-6-5

    (c) 2-4-1-3-6-8-5-7

    (d) 1-3-2-8-5-6-7-4

GO ON TO THE NEXT PAGE.

7. Arrange the following sentences in proper order to create a succinct, well-written paragraph.

(1) An employee's personal problems should become the supervisor's business when (a) the problem impacts on the employee's work, or (b) the employee asks for the supervisor's help, or (c) the employee's problem results in a personnel complaint.

(2) Their responsibility to counsel subordinates experiencing personal problems is obscured by two common misconceptions: (a) that an employee's personal problems are not the supervisor's business, and (b) that supervisory counseling involves professional therapy.

(3) Of all the roles of the supervisor, that of counselor is least understood by supervisors themselves.

(4) Under any of these circumstances, the supervisor is obligated to counsel the subordinate.

    (a) 1-2-3-4

    (b) 3-2-1-4

    (c) 3-2-4-1

    (d) 4-3-1-2

GO ON TO THE NEXT PAGE.

8. Arrange the following sentences in proper order to create a succinct, well-written paragraph.

(1) By statute, a person "holding any public office, position or employment" must forfeit such office or position if he or she is convicted of an offense involving dishonesty or of a crime of the third degree or above.

(2) Forfeiture of Public Office is a very serious penalty that a police officer pays for unlawful behavior.

(3) In addition, the statute provides that such officer will be required to forfeit his or her office upon conviction of an offense involving or "touching" such office, position or employment.

(4) According to the court, "when the infraction casts such a shadow over the employee as to make his or her continued service appear incompatible with the traits of trustworthiness, honesty, and obedience to law and order, then forfeiture is appropriate."

(5) The term "touches the office" has been defined broadly by the Court in Moore v. Youth Correctional Institute, where the Court held that the petty disorderly persons offense of harassment committed by a corrections officer against his immediate supervisor qualified for forfeiture.

(6) When a forfeiture of office does relate to an offense involving or touching on the person's public office, position or employment, that person shall be forever disqualified from holding any such public office or public position of honor, trust or profit in this State.

    (a) 2-1-3-5-4-6

    (b) 4-5-1-2-3-6

    (c) 1-2-5-4-6-3

    (d) 1-3-4-5-2-6

GO ON TO THE NEXT PAGE.

9. Arrange the following sentences in proper order to create a succinct, well-written paragraph.

(1) Dictators sow seeds of distrust; employees can sense this and will resent it.

(2) The way supervisors exert this authority impacts supervisor-subordinate relationships. The quickest way to alienate subordinates is to act like a dictator.

(3) Authority is the power to command others.

(4) Therefore, a new supervisor should not seek to prove to his subordinates how much he knows during his first few days on the job.

(5) By virtue of their position, supervisors have the authority to issue orders and give instructions to subordinates.

(6) Instead, he should spend this time learning about his subordinates and seeking their advice.

    (a) 1-2-4-3-5-6

    (b) 5-4-3-1-2-6

    (c) 3-5-6-4-2-1

    (d) 3-5-2-1-4-6

10. Arrange the following sentences in proper order to create a succinct, well-written paragraph.

(1) If the law is to be honored, it must first be honored by those who enforce it.

(2) Quite the contrary, the use of illegal means, no matter how worthy the end, is certain to encourage disrespect for the law and its officers.

(3) Law enforcement officers should not subscribe to the idea that the end justifies the means.

(4) This will then provide an impetus for those in the community to follow suit.

    (a) 1-2-3-4

    (b) 2-3-1-4

    (c) 3-2-1-4

    (d) 3-4-1-2

END OF EXERCISE

1. (b) **3-1-2-4.** At 3:00 p.m., Mike Johnson broke into a green, two-door Ford. He then started the car by "hot wiring" the ignition. Johnson drove off at a high rate of speed. Officer Jones witnessed the entire event and closely followed Johnson.

2. (b) **2-4-1-3-5.** Over-supervision is the most common error made by new supervisors. In their zeal to get the job done, they forget that their new position requires them to delegate authority to their subordinates. Instead, they become overly involved in controlling the routine activities of their subordinates and, even worse, they do the actual work themselves, often under the mistaken belief that they will win the favor of their subordinates. However, most workers resent such an approach and often view it as indicative of a lack of confidence in their abilities. To complicate the matter even more, over-supervision also curtails worker initiative, creates morale problems and decreases respect for the supervisor.

3. (c) **1-5-2-4-3.** Very few officers have the ability to recall from memory all the details of a complex case or incident several hours, days or months later, when it becomes necessary to prepare a formal report or testify in court. While there is no need to record every single detail about an incident in your field notebook, you should record enough detail about the incident to refresh your memory of related facts. In this respect, the notes you record in your field notebook may be considered an "index" to your memory. With practice, you will develop a form of shorthand that will assist you in quickly recording the relevant details of an event without the need to overload pages with unnecessary words. Above all else, the notes you record in your field notebook should be accurate, clear and concise.

4. (d) **3-1-2.** Many officers fall into the trap of believing that sketches are not necessary when the crime scene is being processed and photographed by crime-scene personnel. This is dead wrong. As a demonstrative form of evidence, the crime-scene sketch provides a graphic display of the scene (in whole or in part) with accurate measurements of distances between objects.

5. (c) **2-4-1-3.** The hallmark of the competent law enforcement officer is the ability to record his or her observations in a clear, concise and readily understandable manner. One of the means through which an officer's observations and actions are recorded is the "Incident" or "Operations Report." Another is the "Investigation" or "Supplementary Investigation Report." These are the official documents which provide the spark which fires the other components of the criminal justice system into action.

6. (a) **1-8-3-5-6-2-7-4.** On July 3, 2001, at 12:20 p.m., I, Officer Brent Young, was dispatched to 123 Main Street in reference to a call of a "man down and bleeding." The building at 123 Main Street is a three-story apartment building. Upon my arrival at 123 Main Street, I was met by the building superintendent, Lonny Anderson. He stated that while he was eating lunch, he heard a loud thud in the hallway of the building. He then immediately looked out his door and saw his neighbor, Gregg Samson, lying on the floor. At the time, Samson was bleeding from his forehead. I approached Samson and asked what had happened. He stated that he wasn't watching where he was walking and tripped down the stairs.

7. (b) **3-2-1-4.** Of all the roles of the supervisor, the role of counselor is least understood by supervisors themselves. Their responsibility to counsel subordinates experiencing personal problems is obscured by two common misconceptions: (a) that an employee's personal problems are not the supervisor's business, and (b) that supervisory counseling involves professional therapy. An employee's personal problems should become the supervisor's business when (a) the problem impacts on the employee's work, or (b) the employee asks for the supervisor's help, or (c) the employee's problem results in a personnel complaint. Under any of these circumstances, the supervisor is obligated to counsel the subordinate.

8. (a) **2-1-3-5-4-6.** Forfeiture of Public Office is a very serious penalty that a police officer pays for unlawful behavior. By statute, a person "holding any public office, position or employment" must forfeit such office or position if he or she is convicted of an offense involving dishonesty or of a crime of the third degree or above. In addition, the statute provides that such officer will be required to forfeit his or her office upon conviction of an offense involving or "touching" such office, position or employment. The term "touches the office" has been defined broadly by the Court in *Moore v. Youth Correctional Institute*, where the Court held that the petty disorderly persons offense of harassment committed by a corrections officer against his immediate supervisor qualified for forfeiture. According to the court, "when the infraction casts such a shadow over the employee as to make his or her continued service appear incompatible with the traits of trustworthiness, honesty, and obedience to law and order, then forfeiture is appropriate." When a forfeiture of office does relate to an offense involving or touching on the person's public office, position or employment, that person shall be forever disqualified from holding any such public office or public position of honor, trust or profit in this State.

9. (d) **3-5-2-1-4-6.** Authority is the power to command others. By virtue of their position, supervisors have the authority to issue orders and give instructions to subordinates. The way supervisors exert this authority impacts supervisor-subordinate relationships. The quickest way to alienate subordinates is to act like a dictator. Dictators sow seeds of distrust; employees can sense this and will resent it. Therefore, a new supervisor should not seek to prove to his subordinates how much he knows during his first few days on the job. Instead, he should spend this time learning about his subordinates and seeking their advice.

10. (c) **3-2-1-4.** Law enforcement officers should not subscribe to the idea that the end justifies the means. Quite the contrary, the use of illegal means, no matter how worthy the end, is certain to encourage disrespect for the law and its officers. If the law is to be honored, it must first be honored by those who enforce it. This will then provide an impetus for those in the community to follow suit.

Notes

1. You will find it helpful, when sitting down to write your report, to begin with a kind of image—a picture to carry in your mind's eye. That picture should be of

    (a) the time needed to write the report.

    (b) the person or group of people who will be reading your report.

    (c) the next event that needs to be properly recorded.

    (d) when the report will need to be filed.

2. To properly maintain perspective when writing a police report, you should ask yourself three questions. Which is not one of those questions?

    (a) How much time do I have to write this report?

    (b) In what way will this report become a part of a future proceeding?

    (c) Who is my audience?

    (d) Why am I writing this report?

3. Prior to writing a formal police report, you should think through each portion of the report from beginning to end. This will assist in providing

    (a) completeness and reason.

    (b) clarity and coherence.

    (c) style and grammar.

    (d) ambiguity and reason.

GO ON TO THE NEXT PAGE.

4. An essential element of Effective Law Enforcement Reporting is "completeness." Which statement provides a correct instruction in this regard? When writing your report you should

(a) include all material that is competent but not relevant.

(b) include evidence even if you think it is inadmissible.

(c) include all information that is relevant but not material.

(d) tell the reader that more information is needed.

5. It is imperative for all officers to recognize the importance and purpose of official reports. The central purpose of reports is to

(a) provide a formal basis for a supplemental report.

(b) provide a written record of your opinions.

(c) communicate information.

(d) allow an incident to be recorded without too much detail.

6. Simple notations made in the field that serve as a shorthand or abbreviated written record of what was seen, said or done are called

(a) crime-scene records.

(b) incident reports.

(c) field notes.

(d) investigation reports.

7. An officer's field notebook serves as the Department's

(a) official memory.

(b) transcription account.

(c) field statistics

(d) unofficial memory.

GO ON TO THE NEXT PAGE.

8. Which of the below MOST accurately completes the following sentence? Studies have shown that the mere act of _____ will impress the event more deeply in the person's memory.

    (a) thinking about something

    (b) writing something down

    (c) saying, "remember this"

    (d) saying something twice

9. As a general matter, field notes need not *always* be saved for future proceedings. So long as you carefully and fully incorporate your field notes into your formal report, the field notes may be discarded. Two words of caution: First, although there is no general legal mandate calling for the preservation of most forms of field notes, your department may have a rule or regulation requiring it. Second, as a matter of standard practice and procedure, many law enforcement agencies and courts require the retention of an officer's or agent's "rough notes" which

    I.   document an interview with a prospective witness.

    II.   contain information that is exculpatory in nature.

    III. contain information that is favorable and material to the defense.

    IV. contain abbreviations.

Which statements are MOST correct?

    (a) I and II only.

    (b) II and III only.

    (c) I, II and III only.

    (d) I, II, III and IV.

GO ON TO THE NEXT PAGE.

10. Officer Swells asks you what the most appropriate way would be to handle note taking during the course of a street interview. Your best advice would be:

    I.   Don't take notes until the subject identifies himself.

    II. To allay any suspicions about note taking, the interviewer should always briefly explain to the subject at the start of the interview that the notes are meant to prevent subsequent re-interviews brought on by the inability of the interviewer to remember all of the pertinent facts discussed.

    III. Don't get so caught up in taking notes that you fail to show interest in the immediate discussion.

    IV. If the subject adamantly objects to the taking of notes during the interview, try to conduct the interview without taking notes.

    (a) I and II only are correct.

    (b) II and III only are correct.

    (c) I, II and IV only are correct.

    (d) I, II, III and IV are correct.

11. "Completeness" is an important factor in any good report. Which statement best reflects this principle?

    (a) Include facts about the witness' background, if they reflect on his credibility.

    (b) When writing the report, you should include everything the witness said.

    (c) The reader's knowledge should be taken for granted.

    (d) When writing the report, include only those comments made by the witness which are direct quotes.

GO ON TO THE NEXT PAGE.

12. Effective report writing is an important attribute for any officer to have. Which statement set forth below is the most accurate concerning the format of a good report?

(a) Important sentences should be placed in the middle of the report so that the reader does not miss them.

(b) Topic headings should be omitted because they destroy the unity of the report.

(c) Lengthy and repetitious descriptions of documents should be avoided by using columnar tabulation whenever you describe a group of items having similar characteristics.

(d) Comments should be inserted to explain the importance of critical events.

13. When officers write reports with short sentences and short paragraphs, those reports are

(a) too simple for effective reporting.

(b) easy to read, and less time is required to study and comprehend the material.

(c) usually missing critical information which is necessary for formal documentation.

(d) generally invalid and should not be used as a basis for supplementary reports.

14. When writing a formal report, an officer should avoid using superlatives

(a) unless the officer can quote them verbatim.

(b) because they tend to interfere with the report's relevance.

(c) unless they have been verified through independent investigation.

(d) because the reader may doubt the writer's objectivity.

GO ON TO THE NEXT PAGE.

15. Crime-scene sketches not only assist an officer when writing the formal report, but they

(a) also serve as a unique documentary exhibit at trial.

(b) may not be used at trial.

(c) cannot be referred to at a later date.

(d) also are a non-discoverable piece of evidence for the prosecution.

16. The crime-scene sketch provides a graphic display of the scene (in whole or in part) with accurate measurements of distances between objects. The sketch helps create a mental picture of the scene for those who were not present, and also assists officers in a number of other ways. Which statement is LEAST accurate? Crime scene sketches

I. assist in accurately portraying the physical facts of the incident and in relating the sequence of events at the scene.

II. can establish the precise location and relationship of objects and evidence at the scene.

III. assist in interviewing and interrogating persons connected with the crime or incident.

IV. create a permanent record of the scene and assist in presenting the case in court.

V. at times, tend to distort angles and relationships between objects and evidence.

(a) I, IV and V only.

(b) II and IV only.

(c) III only.

(d) V only.

17. The preliminary crime-scene sketch drawn by the investigator or crime-scene technician as he or she takes field notes is the first diagram of the scene and is generally not drawn to scale. This sketch is called the

(a) finished crime-scene sketch.

(b) unfinished sketch.

(c) rough crime-scene sketch.

(d) preliminary detailed sketch.

GO ON TO THE NEXT PAGE.

18. Which method of crime-scene sketching is an easy method for locating objects and evidence in a square or rectangular room; employs two adjacent walls as fixed points from which distances are measured at right angles; and locates objects by measuring from one wall at right angles and then from the adjacent wall at right angles?

(a) The rectangular-coordinate method.

(b) The baseline method.

(c) The triangulation method.

(d) The cross projection method.

19. Which method of crime-scene sketching is used most often in outdoor settings where there are no readily identifiable reference points, such as edges of fields or roads, to use as baselines?

(a) The rectangular-coordinate method.

(b) The baseline method.

(c) The triangulation method.

(d) The cross projection method.

20. Which method of crime-scene sketching is used when it is necessary to locate objects on walls or show the relationship between evidence on the floor and evidence on the walls? This sketch is drawn as though the viewer is straight above it, looking down at it; in effect, the room is flattened out like a box cut down at the four corners and opened flat.

(a) The rectangular-coordinate method.

(b) The baseline method.

(c) The triangulation method.

(d) The cross projection method.

21. Which sketch is useful for illustrating a significant chain of events, for example, the path of a bullet, or movement of suspects, victims or vehicles?

(a) The schematic sketch.

(b) The elevation sketch.

(c) The triangulation sketch.

(d) The cross projection sketch.

GO ON TO THE NEXT PAGE.

22. Law enforcement reports should be "coherent." "Coherence" is the quality of

(a) conciseness.

(b) logic and order.

(c) brevity.

(d) subjectivity.

23. The use of which of the following tools strengthens report writing skills, assists in organizing the information that must be reported and serves as an abstract of the critical facts that must be documented in the formal report?

(a) a proof reader

(b) an outline

(c) a tape recorder

(d) a Dictaphone

24. Proper use of the tool identified in the last question also helps in each of the following ways, except:

(a) It helps to ensure the completeness of your final report.

(b) It helps you to avoid rambling on about unimportant matters.

(c) It helps you to stick to and focus on the facts.

(d) It must be used at trial.

25. It is well known that the preliminary steps taken at the scene of a crime guard against improper actions and mistakes. Prior to taking notes, when processing a crime scene for clues and evidence, which of the following BEST describes the first step the officer should take? The officer should

(a) identify the perpetrators, if any.

(b) conduct an analysis of the information obtained.

(c) conduct a survey of the surroundings and an evaluation of the situation.

(d) coordinate full and complete interviews and interrogations.

GO ON TO THE NEXT PAGE.

26. Field interviews have several principal objectives. Which of the below LEAST accurately sets forth one of the principal objectives of having a department-wide, organized field interview program?

    (a) identification

    (b) prevention and repression of crime

    (c) centralized records of field contacts.

    (d) officer accountability.

27. Your supervisor has just handed you a report written by one of your subordinates regarding a prisoner who had escaped two days ago. He asks that you carefully read the report and go over the officer's report-writing problems with him. As you review the report, you notice a number of defects regarding the time and place of occurrence, along with other missing pieces of information, such as who initially reported the matter, what actions were initially taken, and so on. Your most appropriate course of action at this point would be to make sure that the officer

    (a) is told to rewrite the report and to include the "when, where, why and how" of report writing.

    (b) and all the other officers are given in-service training in the proper way to write reports.

    (c) is disciplined for his inept report writing.

    (d) is instructed to describe the incident in terms of the who, what, when, where, why, and how of report writing.

28. During the course of a police academy class on "Report Writing," the instructor emphasized that police reports must be written in a fair and impartial way. This means that an officer's report should not be influenced by emotion, bias or prejudice, and should not be opinionated. In a word, police reports should be

    (a) subjective.

    (b) objective.

    (c) partial.

    (d) static.

GO ON TO THE NEXT PAGE.

29. When writing an official report, officers should follow some basic rules. Consider these statements.

    I.   Officers should record all relevant facts and strive for accuracy.

    II. Officers should avoid legal conclusions.

    III. Officers should fully document their sources of information.

    IV. Information from anonymous tips require the least amount of independent verification.

    V. Officers should use shorthand expressions whenever possible.

Which statements are LEAST correct?

    (a) II and IV only.

    (b) IV only.

    (c) V only.

    (d) IV and V only.

30. Whenever you write a formal report, it is a good idea to do each of the following, except

    (a) set it aside for a few minutes before proof reading it because most persons are initially "word blind" to their own material.

    (b) immediately submit your report for case filing as soon as you finish writing it.

    (c) in more involved or more serious cases, preview the facts and circumstances of the case with the investigator or detective before you begin the process of drafting your report.

    (d) insist on investigatory or supervisory review of the report before submitting it for case filing.

END OF EXERCISE

1. (b) You will find it helpful, when sitting down to write your report, to begin with a kind of image—a picture to carry in your mind's eye. That picture should be of *the person or group of people who will be reading your report.*

2. (a) To properly maintain perspective when writing a police report, you should ask yourself three questions: *Why am I writing this report? Who is my audience?* and *In what way will this report become part of a future proceeding?*

3. (b) Prior to writing a formal police report, you should think through each portion of the report from beginning to end. This will assist in providing *clarity and coherence.*

4. (b) An essential element of Effective Law Enforcement Reporting is "completeness." When writing your report you should *include evidence even if you think it is inadmissible.* A court will ultimately decide what is or is not admissible.

5. (c) It is imperative for all officers to recognize the importance and purpose of official reports. The central purpose of reports is to *communicate information.*

6. (c) Simple notations made in the field that serve as a shorthand or abbreviated written record of what was seen, said or done are called *field notes.*

7. (a) An officer's field notebook serves as the Department's *"official memory."*

8. (b) Which of the below MOST accurately completes the following sentence? Studies have shown that the mere act of *writing something down* will impress the event more deeply in the person's memory.

9. (c) Although there is no general legal mandate calling for the preservation of most forms of field notes, your department may have a rule or regulation requiring it. Second, as a matter of standard practice and procedure, many law enforcement agencies and courts require the retention of an officer's or agent's "rough notes" which I. document an interview with a prospective witness; II. contain information that is exculpatory in nature; or III. contain information that is favorable and material to the defense.

10. (d) You should tell Officer Swells all of the following: I. Don't take notes until the subject identifies himself; II. To allay any suspicions about note taking, the interviewer should always briefly explain to the subject at the start of the interview that the notes are meant to prevent subsequent re-interviews brought on by the inability of the interviewer to remember all of the pertinent facts discussed; III. Don't get so caught up in taking notes that you fail to show interest in the immediate discussion; and IV. If the subject adamantly objects to the taking of notes during the interview, try to conduct the interview without taking notes.

11. (a) "Completeness" is an important factor in any good report. In this respect, the report writer should: *Include facts about the witness' background, if they reflect on his credibility.*

12. (c) Effective report writing is an important attribute for any officer to have. Concerning the format of a good report, the following statement is most accurate: *Lengthy and repetitious descriptions of documents should be avoided by using columnar tabulation whenever you describe a group of items having similar characteristics.*

13. (b) When officers write reports with short sentences and short paragraphs, those reports are *easy to read, and less time is required to study and comprehend the material.*

14. (d) When writing a formal report, an officer should avoid using superlatives because *the reader may doubt the writer's objectivity.*

15. (a) Crime-scene sketches not only assist an officer when writing the formal report, but they *also serve as a unique documentary exhibit at trial.*

16. (d) Crime-scene sketches I. assist in accurately portraying the physical facts of the incident and in relating the sequence of events at the scene; II. can establish the precise location and relationship of objects and evidence at the scene; III. assist in interviewing and interrogating persons connected with the crime or incident; and IV. create a permanent record of the scene and assist in presenting the case in court. Statement V. is incorrect. *Photographs*, not sketches, at times tend to distort angles and relationships between objects and evidence.

17. (c) The preliminary crime-scene sketch drawn by the investigator or crime-scene technician as he or she takes field notes is the first diagram of the scene and is generally not drawn to scale. This sketch is called the *rough crime-scene sketch*.

18. (a) *The rectangular-coordinate method* of crime-scene sketching is an easy method for locating objects and evidence in a square or rectangular room. It employs two adjacent walls as fixed points from which distances are measured at right angles, and locates objects by measuring from one wall at right angles and then from the adjacent wall at right angles.

19. (c) *The triangulation method* of crime-scene sketching is used most often in outdoor settings where there are no readily identifiable reference points, such as edges of fields or roads, to use as baselines.

20. (d) *The cross projection method* of crime-scene sketching is used when it is necessary to locate objects on walls or show the relationship between evidence on the floor and evidence on the walls. This sketch is drawn as though the viewer is straight above it, looking down at it; in effect, the room is flattened out like a box cut down at the four corners and opened flat.

21. (a) *The schematic sketch* is useful for illustrating a significant chain of events, for example, the path of a bullet, or movement of suspects, victims or vehicles.

22. (b) Law enforcement reports should be "coherent." "Coherence" is the quality of *logic and order.*

23. (b) The use of *an outline* strengthens report writing skills, assists in organizing the information that must be reported and serves as an abstract of the critical facts that must be documented in the formal report?

24. (d) Properly *outlining* your observations and actions helps you (a) to ensure the completeness of your final report; (b) to avoid rambling on about unimportant matters; and (c) to stick to and focus on the facts. There is no requirement that the outline be saved for, or used at, trial.

25. (c) Prior to taking notes, when processing a crime scene for clues and evidence, which of the following BEST describes the first step the officer should take? The officer should *conduct a survey of the surroundings and an evaluation of the situation.*

26. (d) Officer accountability is not one of the principal objectives of having a department-wide, organized field interview program. Those objectives include: (a) *identification;* (b) *prevention and repression of crime;* and (c) *centralized records of field contacts.*

27. (d) In this report, you notice a number of defects regarding *when* and *where* the incident occurred, along with other missing pieces of information, such as *who* initially reported the matter, *what* actions were initially taken, and so on. Your most appropriate course of action at this point would be to make sure that the officer *is instructed to describe the incident in terms of the who, what, when, where, why, and how of report writing.* Choice (b) is not correct, for it would not be wise to expend resources in training *all the other officers* when only one officer is shown to have the report-writing problem.

28. (b) Police reports should be written in a fair and impartial way. This means that an officer's report should not be influenced by emotion, bias or prejudice, and should not be opinionated. In a word, police reports should be *objective.*

29. (d) When writing an official report, officers should follow some basic rules. The following statements are *correct*: I. Officers should record all relevant facts and strive for accuracy; II. Officers should avoid legal conclusions; and III. Officers should fully document their sources of information. Statement IV. is not correct, for information from anonymous tips requires the MOST amount of independent verification. Also, statement V. is not correct, for officers should AVOID using shorthand expressions. They are a poor replacement for the factual detail which they circumvent.

30. (b) It is a bad idea to immediately submit a police report for case filing *as soon as it is finished*. Rather, whenever you write a formal report, it is a good idea to (a) set it aside for a few minutes before proof reading it because most persons are initially "word blind" to their own material; in more involved or more serious cases, preview the facts and circumstances of the case with the investigator or detective *before* you begin the process of drafting your report; and (d) insist on investigatory or supervisory review of the report before submitting it for case filing.

Notes

PART III
EFFECTIVE LAW
ENFORCEMENT REPORTING
REFERENCE SECTION

accede....................................to comply
exceed................................... to surpass

accent..........................stress in speech
or writing
ascent .... act of rising
assent ....consent

accept .... to take
or receive
except ....to exclude

access...................................admittance
excess.. surplus

ad .... short for
advertisement
add .... to join,
unite, combine

adapt .... to adjust
adept .... proficient
adopt...................................... to choose

addition ....something
added
edition............................one version of
a printed work

adverse ....harmful;
hostile; unfavorable
averse ....opposed to

advice ....(n.) information;
recommendation
advise ....(v.) to recommend;
to give counsel

affect............................. to influence; to
change; to assume
effect............... (n.) result; impression;
(v.) to bring about

aid .... (n.) a form of help;
(v.) to help
aide.................................... an assistant

allot.................................... to assign or
distribute a share
of something
a lot ....a great deal;
do not use "alot"

allowed .... permitted
aloud..audibly

almost .... nearly
all most..........................all very much

PART III

269

already .... previously
all ready ....all prepared

---

altar .... part of a church
alter .... to change

---

alternate....................... (n.) substitute;
(v.) to take turns
alternative.......................one of several
things to choose
from

---

altogether...................................entirely
all together........... everyone in a group

---

appraise...................... to set a value on
apprise .... to inform

---

assure .... to give confidence
to another
ensure...........................to make certain
insure .... to protect
against loss

---

bail .... (n.) security; the
handle of a pail;
(v.) to dip water
bale...a bundle

---

baloney ....nonsense
bologna.......................smoked sausage

---

bare ....(adj.) naked; empty;
(v.) to expose
bear .... (n.) an animal;
(v.) to carry, produce, endure

beat .... (n.) throb; tempo;
(v.) to strike
beet..................................... a vegetable

---

berth.. a bed
birth .... being born

---

beside............................ by the side of,
separate from
besides ....in addition
to; also

---

better...............................greater than;
more effective
bettor.............................. one who bets

---

bizarre.....................................fantastic;
extravagantly odd
bazaar............................a place to sell
merchandise

---

born .... brought into life
borne.......................... carried; endured

---

brake ....(n.) a retarding device;
(v.) to retard
break ....(n.) opening; fracture;
(v.) to shatter, divide

---

breath.............................. respiration
breathe ....to inhale and exhale
breadth...width

---

calendar .... a record of time
calender ....machine used in
finishing paper or cloth

canvas............................a coarse cloth
canvass ....to solicit

capital .... (n.) city serving as the seat
of government; a principal
sum of money; an
upper-case letter;
(adj.) chief; fore-most;
punishable by death
capitol .... the building in which a
legislative body meets

caret................... a wedge-shaped mark
carat............................ a unit of weight
for precious stones
karat .... a unit of fineness
for gold

cash ....ready money
cache .... a place for hiding
or storing items

casual .... informal; occasional
causal .... causing

cereal.................food made from grain
serial........... (adj.) arranged in a series;
(n.) a work appearing in
parts or at intervals

cite................................ (v.) to quote; to
summon sight
a view; vision
site..a place
sight................................. ability to see;
field of vision

clench........................ to bring together
tightly; close
clinch .... to fix, secure or
fasten; to settle definitely

coarse .... rough; common
course........................ direction; action;
a way; part of a meal

coma .... an unconscious state
comma............. a mark of punctuation

command .... (n.) an order, or
assignment; (v.) to order
commend............. to praise; to entrust

complement ....something
that completes
compliment... (n.) a flattering remark;
(v.) to praise

confidant................a friend; an adviser
confident...........................sure; positive

conscience.........................the sense of
right and wrong
conscious .... cognizant; aware

continual........... occurring steadily but
with occasional
interruptions
continuous...uninterrupted; unbroken

correspondence ....written
communication
correspondents..........those who write;
journalists
corespondents ....certain parties in
lawsuits

PART III

council ....legislative body; an assembly

counsel...........(n.) an attorney; advice; (v.) to give advice

consul.............a foreign representative

———

courtesy................... a favor, politeness

curtesy...............husband's life interest in the lands of his deceased wife

curtsy......................a gesture of respect

———

credible ....believable

creditable ....meritorious; deserving of praise

———

critic ....one who makes judgments

critique.........(n.) a critical assessment; (v.) to judge;

———

dairy .... source of milk products

diary .... a record kept on a regular basis

———

decent........................... proper, correct

descent ....going down

dissent........disagreement; disapproval

———

deference.......................respect; regard for another's wishes

difference .....dissimilarity; controversy

———

defuse................to make less harmful; to make less tense

diffuse .... wordy; badly organized

———

deposition.............. a formal statement usually under oath

disposition.................temper; disposal

depraved ....morally debased

deprived...........................left without; taken away from

———

desert..........................(n.) barren land; (plural) a deserved reward; (v.) to abandon

dessert .... the last course of a meal

———

device .... a contrivance

devise .... to plan; to convey real estate by will

———

die ....(n.) mold; (v.) to cease living

dye................................ (n.) that which changes the color of; (v.) to change the color of

———

disburse...............................to pay out

disperse....................................to scatter

———

discreet.................................... prudent

discrete......................distinct; separate

———

divers............. (adj.) various or sundry; (n.) plural of diver

diverse................................... different

———

dual ....double

duel .... a combat

———

dying ....near death

dyeing .... changing the color of an item

———

elicit .... to draw forth

illicit...unlawful

eligible ....qualified
illegible ....unreadable

emerge........................... to rise out of
immerge........................to plunge into

emigrate ....to leave a country
immigrate ....to enter a country

eminent..........well-known; prominent
imminent.......threatening; impending

envelop .... (v.) to cover; to wrap
envelope ....(n.) a container for
a letter

expand .... to increase in size
expend .... to spend

explicit ....clearly expressed
implicit .... implied

facet....................................... an aspect
faucet.. a tap

facilitate .... to make easy
felicitate .... to congratulate

faint...........................(adj.) dim; weak;
(v.) to pass out
feint.............. a trick; a deceptive move

fair......................(adj.) favorable; just;
(n.) an exhibit
fare ....(n.) cost of travel;
food; (v.) to go forth

farther ....at a greater distance;
referring to actual distance
further .....to a greater extent or degree;
moreover; in addition

flair...aptitude
flare ....a light or signal

flew...did fly
flue .... a chimney
flu ....short for influenza

formally ....in a formal manner
formerly .... came before

forth .... away; forward
fourth.................... 4th, next after third

forward ....ahead
foreword ....preface

gage ....pledge, token of defiance
gauge........................measuring device

genius.................................... very smart
genus........................a classification in
botany or zoology

grate .... (n.) a frame of bars;
(v.) to scrape; to irritate
great ....large; magnificent

guarantee .... an assurance
guaranty .... a promise to answer
for the debt of another

_____

hangar .... a building for aircraft
hanger .... a device to hang
items like clothing

_____

higher .... at a greater height
hire .... to employ; to use
the services of another

_____

holy .... sacred
holey .... full of holes
wholly .... entirely
holly .... a tree

_____

human .... pertaining to humanity
humane .... kindly

_____

hurdle .... an obstacle, barrier
or difficulty
hurtle .... to throw or fling
with great force

_____

illicit .... unlawful
elicit .... to draw forth

_____

imitate .... to resemble; to mimic
intimate .... (adj.) innermost;
familiar; (v.) to hint;
to make known

_____

imply .... to suggest
infer .... to deduce; to guess;
to conclude

incidence .... range of occurrence
incidents .... occurrences; happenings

_____

incinerate .... to burn
insinuate .... to imply

_____

incite .... to arouse
insight .... understanding

_____

indict .... to charge with a crime
indite .... to compose; to write

_____

ingenious .... clever
ingenuous .... naive
disingenuous .... pretending to
be naive

_____

insoluble .... incapable of
being dissolved
insolvable .... not explainable

_____

instants .... short periods of time
instance .... an example

_____

intense .... acute; strong
intents .... aims

_____

isle .... island
aisle .... passage between rows

_____

its .... possessive form of it
it's .... contraction of it is or it has

_____

knew .... understood
new .... fresh; novel

lapse .... to become void
elapse .... to pass
relapse .... to slip back into
a former condition

lay... to place
lie .... (n.) a falsehood;
(v.) to recline;
to tell an untruth
lye................ a strong alkaline solution

lead......................... (n.) a heavy metal;
(v.) to guide
led .... guided (past tense
of to lead)

lean .... (adj.) thin; (v.) to incline
lien .... a legal claim

leased .... rented
least.. smallest

legislator .... one who writes laws
legislature........... a body of lawmakers

lend .... to allow the use
of temporarily
loan .... (n.) something lent;
(v.) to lend
lone .... solitary

lessee .... a tenant
lesser .... of smaller size
lessor .... one who gives a lease

lessen........................... to make smaller
lesson ....an exercise assigned for study

liable .... responsible
libel .... defamatory statement

lightening...................... making lighter
lightning .... the flash of light that
accompanies thunder
lighting........................... illumination

loose........................ (adj.) not bound;
(v.) to release
lose .... (v.) to suffer a loss of;
to part with unintentionally
loss .... something lost

made .... constructed or created
maid.. a servant

main........... (adj.) chief; (n.) a conduit
mane .... long hair on the
neck of certain animals

manner......................... a way of acting
or doing something
manor .... an estate

marital............. pertaining to marriage
martial............................. military like
marshal .... (n.) an official;
(v.) to arrange

medal .... a badge of honor
meddle.............................. to interfere
metal .... a mineral
mettle.......................... courage; spirit

miner.......... one who works in a mine
minor .... (adj.) lesser in size, extent,
or importance; (n.) a person
who is under legal age

PART III

missal ....a book of prayers
missile .... a rocket or other projectile

_____

mist ....haze
missed .... failed to do

_____

morning............. the time before noon
mourning.. grief

_____

ordinance.............................a local law
ordnance....................arms; munitions

_____

overdo......................... to do too much
overdue ....past due

_____

packed.................................... crowded
pact................................. an agreement

_____

pail ....a bucket
pale.................................... light-colored

_____

pain...suffering
pane .... window glass

_____

pair............................... two of a kind
pare .... to peel, cut
pear ....a fruit

_____

palate .... roof of the mouth;
the sense of taste
pallet..........................a bed; a mattress;
a portable platform for
stacking materials
palette ....a board holding
a painter's pigments;
a range of colors

past........................... (n.) time gone by;
(adj., adv., or prep.) gone by
passed ....moved along;
transferred (past tense of pass)

_____

patience........... composure; endurance
patients .... sick persons

_____

peace .... calmness
piece......................................a portion

_____

peak...the top
peek...........................to look slyly at
pique......................... (n.) resentment;
(v.) to offend; to arouse

_____

pedal .... (adj.) pertaining to the
foot; (n.) a treadle
peddle .... to hawk; to sell

_____

peer ....(n.) one of equal rank
or age; (v.) to look steadily
pier .... a wharf

_____

perfect .... (adj.) without fault;
(v.) to make perfect
prefect ....an official

_____

perpetrate........... to carry out (a crime)
perpetuate.............. to make perpetual

_____

persecute............................... to oppress
prosecute....................... to sue or bring
criminal charges against

_____

personal .... private
personnel .... the staff

perspective .... a view in correct proportion
prospective .... anticipated

pole .... a long, slender piece of wood or metal
poll .... (n.) the casting of votes by a body of persons; (v.) to register votes

portion .... a part
proportion .... a ratio of parts
apportion .... to allot

practicable .... workable; feasible
practical .... useful

precede .... to go before
proceed .... to advance

precedence .... priority
precedents .... established rules or law

prescribe .... to designate
proscribe .... to outlaw

principal .... (adj.) chief; leading; (n.) a capital sum of money that draws interest; chief official of a school
principle .... a general truth; a rule; integrity

quiet .... calm; not noisy
quite .... entirely; wholly
quit .... stop

raze .... to destroy
rays .... beams

rap .... to knock
wrap .... (n.) a garment; (v.) to enclose
rapt .... engrossed
wrapped .... past tense of wrap

real .... actual
reel .... (n.) a dance; (v.) to whirl

reality .... actuality
realty .... real estate

recent .... relating to a time not long past
resent .... to feel hurt by

residence .... a house
residents .... persons who reside in a place

respectably .... in a manner worthy of respect
respectfully ...... in a courteous manner
respectively .... in the order indicated

role .... a part in a play
roll .... (n.) a list; a type of bread; (v.) to revolve

root .... underground part of a plant; to implant firmly
route .... an established course of travel; to send by a certain route
en route .... on or along the way
rout .... confused flight; to defeat

scent ....odor
sent...did send
cent..penny

———

seam ....a connecting line
or location
seem ....to appear

———

shear................................. to cut or trim
sheer...........................transparent; utter

———

shown ....displayed; revealed
shone .... gave off light; did shine

———

soluble .... having the ability
to dissolve in a liquid
solvable...................... capable of being
solved or explained

———

sore.. painful
soar... to fly

———

spacious ....ample room
specious ....outwardly correct but
inwardly false

———

stair ....a step
stare....................................... to look at

———

stake ....a pointed stick; a prize;
to wager
steak ....a slice of meat

———

stationary ....fixed
stationery .... writing materials

statue...........a carved or molded figure
statute..........................a law written by
the legislature

———

steal .... to take unlawfully
steel ....a form of iron

———

straight .... not crooked; directly
strait .... a water passageway

———

suit .... (n.) a legal action;
clothing; (v.) to please
suite..................a group of things (e.g.,
rooms or furniture)
that form a unit
sweet .... having an agreeable
taste; pleasing

———

tail ....the end
tale..a story

———

taught................................... did teach
taut....................................... tight; tense

———

tenant............. one who rents property
tenet ....a principle

———

than ....conjunction of comparison
then................................... at that time

———

their.........................belonging to them
there ....in that place
they're ....contraction of they are

———

throes ....a painful struggle
throws ....hurls; flings

through .... by means of;
from beginning to end;
threw .... did throw
thorough .... exhaustive

———

track .... a trail
tract .... a treatise; a piece of land

———

trial................................... examination;
experiment; hardship
trail... a path

———

undo...................................... to open; to
render ineffective
undue................... improper, excessive

———

urban.................... pertaining to the city
urbane......................... polished; suave

———

vain .... proud; conceited; futile
vane....................... a device that pivots
on an elevated object
vein .... a blood vessel; a
bed of mineral materials

———

veracious................................... truthful
voracious.................................... greedy

———

vial.................. a small flask for liquids
vile.................... disgusting, despicable

———

waist.................. the body's midsection
waste .... needless destruction;
useless consumption;
to expend uselessly

wait .... to stay
weight .... heaviness

———

waive .... to give up
wave .... a billow; a gesture;
to swing back and forth

———

waiver............. the giving up of a claim
waver................................... to hesitate

———

ware.. goods
wear............... to have on; to diminish
were................................ form of to be
we're .... contraction for we are
where .... at the place in which

———

weather ....state of the atmosphere;
make it safely
whether... if

———

whose...................... possessive of who
who's................. contraction of who is
or who has

———

your............................ belonging to you
you're .... contraction of you are

Notes

A

abandon
abscess
absence
academy
accede
accident
access
accessory
accountant
accuse
accidentally
accommodate
acknowledgment
acquaintance
acquiesce
acquire
activate
actor
adjudicate
administrator
admission
admonish
affidavit
afflict
aggressive
aggressor
alarm
alcohol
allegation
alleged
alignment
allowed
all right
altered
ambivalent
ambulance
annual

anonymous
apparatus
apparent
appearance
appellant
application
appropriate
arbitrate
argument
arraignment
arrest
arrived
arson
aspiration
assault
assigned
assistant
assumption
asthma
attacker
attendance
attire
attorney
automobile
auxiliary
aviator
awareness

B

bankruptcy
bargain
bartender
barricaded
battery
because
beneficiary
benefit
benign

bicycle
bizarre
boredom
boundary
bracelet
brochure
buoyant
bureau
burglary

C

cafeteria
calendar
caliber
camaraderie
camera
canceled
cancellation
capital
capitol
captain
catalog
cause
cautious
ceiling
cellular
cemetery
census
chapel
character
chastise
chief
cigar
circular
coincidence
collapse
collateral
collection

PART III

colonel
collaborate
committed
compromise
concede
conceive
condemn
confer
confession
confidential
congested
conscience
conscientious
conscious
consensus
consequence
consciousness
conspiracy
constitution
contribute
contingent
contraband
controlled
convenience
conventional
convicted
counseling
commit
commission
communicate
community
coordinate
complaint
comply
comrade
comprehend
consecutive
contraband
corduroy
corporal
correction
correspondent
counterfeit
courtesy
criminal
custody
custodian
cycle

D

dangerous
defendant
defense
definitely
deliberate
delinquency
delivery
deputy
Des Moines
description
desperately
detective
detrimental
diamond
dilemma
disastrous
discipline
discord
dismantle
dispatch
dispute
dissatisfied
dissimilar
donation
domestic

E

eager
ecstasy
eighth
equipment
embarrass
emphasize
enumerate
erroneous
establish
evacuation
evidential
exaggerate
examiner
exceed
excellent
excessive
exonerate
expectation
experience

expert
explosion
extraordinary

F

fabricate
facilitate
facility
facsimile
failure
familiar
fatigue
February
felony
fibers
fiery
fingerprints
flawless
fluorescent
forbade
foreign
foresee
forfeit
fraudulent
freight
frequently
fulfill

G

general
government
graffiti
gauge
grammar
gray
gruesome
guarantee
guard
guilty

H

handkerchief
harassment
height
hemorrhage
hinder

hindrance
homicide
homogeneous
horrendous
horrible
hors d'oeuvre
haphazard
hilarious
hygiene

I

idiosyncrasy
ignorant
illegal
immediate
impaired
impale
impasse
implementation
impostor
inasmuch as
incarcerate
incident
incision
indict
indictment
indigent
indispensable
influence
information
informant
injury
innocent
innocuous
innuendo
inoculate
inspector
instigate
insurance
intelligence
intercede
interrogation
interview
intoxicant
intoxicate
invasion
investigation
investigator

involvement
irrelevant
itinerary

J

jargon
jealous
jeopardy
jewelry
judgment
juvenile

K

kidnaping
  or kidnapping
khaki
knife

L

labeled
laboratory
laceration
lament
larceny
league
leisure
libel
liaison
license
lien
lieutenant
liquify
litigation
location
loyalty

M

magistrate
maintenance
manager
maneuver
manufacturer
marshaled
mediocre
merchandise

mileage
miniature
minuscule
miscellaneous
mnemonic
mobility
monetary
monitor
mortgage
mounted
minimum
mitigate
murder
muscular

N

narrative
narcotics
necessary
negative
negotiate
neither
niece
ninety
noticeable
nuance

O

observe
obsolescent
obstruct
offender
offense
officer
omit
omission
opposite
ostracize

P

pamphlet
paradigm
parallel
parole
participate
particular

PART III

patience
performance
permissible
perseverance
personal
personnel
persuade
pessimistic
phenomenal
phony
physician
plaintiff
pneumonia
politician
practically
preceding
precede
precipitation
prejudice
prevention
pretense
principal
principle
privilege
probable
procedure
proceed
projectile
promotion
prosecutor
prostitution
protection
psychological
pursue
pursuit

Q

quaint
qualified
quantity
query
quell
question
questionnaire
quiet
quintessential
quite

R

radio
rarely
rational
rationale
reasonable
recede
receive
reckless
recommend
reconnaissance
reconnoiter
recruit
register
registration
regulations
relevant
religion
remedies
rendezvous
reparations
replenish
replicate
rescind
rescue
residue
resistance
responded
responsibility
restaurant
restitution
restoration
review
revocation
revoke
rifle
rigorous
routinely
roster

S

schedule
scissors
search
secede
seize
separate

serology
sergeant
serious
sheriff
sieve
similar
simultaneous
situation
skillful
souvenir
specialist
specimen
statute
statutory
substance
subpoena
subtly
succeed
success
superior
supersede
supervisor
surgeon
surreptitious
surveillance
suspect
suspicious
suspension
synagogue

T

tardy
technical
technician
technique
telephone
terrain
terrible
theater
theft
thorough
threshold
timely
totaled
totality
tourist
tragedy
traveling

trespasser
typical

U

unbelievable
undercover
uniformity
unique
unmanageable
usually
utter

V

vaccinate
vacillate
vacuum
valuable
various
vegetable
vehicular

velocity
vendor
verification
video
vinyl
violation
violator
violence
vocabulary

W

wallet
wandering
warrant
warrantee
weapon
weird
whether
wholly
witness
wonderful

X

Xanax
Xerox
X-ray

Y

yield
yesterday
youngster
youth

Z

zany
zeal
zealousness
zero

PART III

Notes

COMMON ROOTS AND THEIR MEANINGS

Root	Meaning	Example
act, ag	perform, do, drive,	actor, action
am, ami	love, like	amiable, amorous
anim	mind, life, spirit,	animus, animal
annu, enni	yearly	annual
auc, aug	to originate, to increase	augment
aud	hear	audible
bas	low	basement, debase
bene	good, well, gentle	beneficial, benign
bio	life	biology, biography
biblio	book	bibliophile (book collector)
brev	short	abbreviate
cap	seize or hold	capture
ceas, ceed	go, yield	exceed
cent	hundred	century, centipede
chron	time	chronological
clam	shout	clamor
cogn	to know	recognize; cognizant
corp	body	corpse; corporate
cre, cresc	grow	create
cred	trust, believe	credible; incredible
cour, cur	run, course	occur
dec	ten	decade, decimal
dec, dign	suitable	decent
dic, dict	say, speak	dictate; indicate
doc, doct	teach, prove	doctorate; docile
duc	lead	conduct
ego	I, self	egoism, egomaniac
equ	equal	equity, equanimity
ev, et	time, age	medieval
fac, fic	make do, do	difficult
fer	bear, carry	infer
fict, feign	shape, make, fashion	fiction

PART III

Root	Meaning	Example
fid	belief, faith	confide; confidence
fig	shape, form	figure
flu, fluct	flow	fluid
form	shape	format
fort	strong	fortify, fortitude
fract, frai	break	fracture; frail
gen, gin	to give birth, kind	generate
geo	earth	geography
gor	to bring together	category
gree	step	degree
graph, graf	write, draw	autograph, graphic
her, hes	to stick	adhere
ject, jet	to throw	reject
junct	to join	junction
lex, leag, leg	law	legal, legislate
lect, leg, lig	choose, gather, select, read	collect
loc	place, area	location, dislocate
log	say, reason, study	logic
luc, lum, lust	light	illuminate, luster, translucent
man	handle, make,	manage
mem	recall, remember	memory
ment	mind	mental
min	little	minor, minimum
mit, miss	send	transmit, admit
mort	death	mortal, mortician
mot	move	motion
nom	name	nominate
nov	new	novice
oper	work	operate
pass, path	feel, suffer	passion, sympathy
ped	child	pediatrician, pedagogy
ped	foot	peddle, impede
pel, puls	drive, push	propel, repel
pend	to hang, attach	append
phil	love	philosopher
phob	fear	claustrophobia, agoraphobia
phon	sound	phonetic, phonograph
pict	paint, show, draw	picture
pon	put, place	postpone
port	carry	import, export

Root	Meaning	Example
poten	powerful	impotent, potentate, potential
psych	mind	psychology
quir, quer	seek, ask	inquiry, query
rupt	break	disrupt, rupture
sci, scio	to know	conscious
scrib, scrip	write	script
sent, sens	feel, think	sense, sentiment
sequ	follow	sequence
sist	to withstand, be firm	insist
soci	to join, companions	sociable, society
sol	alone	solitary
solv, solu	loosen, explain	solve, dissolve
sop	wisdom	philosophy, sophisticated
spec, spect	look	spectator
spir	breath, soul	respiration
stab, stat	stand, importance	stature
strain, strict	bind, pull	constrict
struct, stroy	build	destroy, destruct
tact, tang	touch	tactile
tele	far away	telescope
tend, tens	stretch, strive	contend
tain	hold, keep	retain, sustain
term	end, boundary, limit	termination, exterminate, terminal
terr	earth	territory
test	see, witness	attest
therm	heat	thermometer
tor, tors	twist	torsion
tract, trai	pull, draw	attract
uni	one	uniform, unite
urb	city	suburban, urban
vac	empty	vacant
ven, vent	come	convene
ver	true	verify, veracity
verb, verv	word	verbal, verbalize
vers, vert	turn, change	versatile
vid, vie, vis	see	visible
vit, viv	live	vital
voc	spoken	vocal
volv, vol	roll, turn	revolve

PART III

COMMON PREFIXES AND THEIR MEANINGS

Prefixes	Meaning	Example
ac-, ad-, af-, ag-,	to, toward, near,	accompany, adjust, affix, aggression
al-, at-	in addition to	allocate, attend
ab-, abs-	away from, off	abrupt, absolve
a-, an-	not, without	apolitical, anemia
ante-	before	anterior
anti-	against	antipathy, antidote
auto-	self	automotive
bi-	two	biped, biennial
cat-, cata-, cath-	down, with	category, catalogue, catheter
circum-	around	circumvent
co-	together, with	cohesiveness, cognate, collaborate
contra-	against, opposite	contradict
de-	opposite, take away from,	decrease
di-, dif-, dis-	apart, separate, two, not	divide, differ, distrust
e-, ex-	out, out of, from	emit, expel
en-, em-	put into	enamor, empower
epi-	upon, beside, over	epilogue
extra-	beyond	extraordinary
il-, im-,	not, in	illegible, illegal, imposter,
in-, ir-	not, in	inaction, irresponsible
inter-	among, between	intercede, interject, international
intro-	into	introspection

Common Prefixes and Meanings

Prefixes	Meaning	Example
mal-	bad	malfunction
mis-	wrong	misconduct
mono-	one	monologue
multi-	many	multiply, multiple
non-	not, no	nonconformist, nonentity, nonsense
ob-, oc-, of-	toward,	obtain, occur, offer
op-	against	oppose
over-	excessive, above	overwork, override
para-	beside	paradox, paraphrase
per-	through	persecute, perforation
post-	after	postpone
pre-	before	precede, preview
pro-	for, forward	propel
re-	back, again	readmit, return, recur, replay, re-act
retro-	backward	retrospect
se-	apart, move away from	secede
semi-	half	semiannual
sub-	under, come after	submarine, subpoena, subvert
suc-	come after	succeed
super-	over, above	superimpose
syn-, sym-	together, at same time	synchronous, synergy, sympathy
trans-	across, beyond, change	transform, transmit, transcend, transport
tri-	three	tripod
un-	not, against, opposite	unavailable, unceasing, unaware
uni-	one	uniform

PART III

COMMON SUFFIXES AND THEIR MEANINGS

Suffixes	Meaning	Example
-able, -ible	capable of being	solvable, combustible, incredible
-acy, -cy	state, quality	privacy, infancy
-age	activity, or result of action	courage
-al (n.)	action	referral
-al, -ial, -ical (adj.)	quality, relation	structural, territorial, categorical
-an	person	artisan, human
-ance, -ence	action, state or process	resistance, abundance, independence
-ancy, -ency	state, quality or capacity	vacancy, agency
-ant, -ent	an agent, actor	disinfectant, aspirant, dependent
-ar, -ary	resembling, related to	spectacular, unitary
-ate (n.)	office, function, one who	candidate, advocate
-ate (v.)	cause to be	graduate
-ation	action, resulting state	specialization
-dom	place, state of being	kingdom, wisdom
-ed	past tense	attained, acquired
-en	to cause, to become	moisten
-er, -or (n.)	one who does something	porter, collector
-er, -or (v.)	to act	ponder, clamor
-est	superlative	strongest, greatest
-fold	in a manner of, marked by	twofold, fourfold
-ful	an amount that fills	mouthful, handful
-fy	cause to be, make	emulsify (make into a milky liquid)
-ia	names, diseases	phobia
-ian	related to, one that is	pedestrian
-iatry	art of healing	psychiatry
-ic, -ics	related to arts, sciences	arithmetic, generic, economics

Common Suffixes and Meanings

Suffixes	Meaning	Example
-ice	act	malice
-ify	cause	specify, vilify
-il, -ile	capable of being	evil, servile, projectile
-ing	material made for, activity	flooring, swimming, building
-ion	condition or action	abduction, adhesion
-ish	having the character of	newish, Jewish
-ism	condition of being	pauperism (being a pauper)
-ism	doctrine, belief, conduct	formalism, tuism
-ist	person or member	podiatrist, ophthalmologist, nudist
-ite	product or part	graphite
-ive, -ative	quality of	festive, predictive, cooperative
-ize	to create, cause	fantasize
-less	without, missing	penniless, relentless, motiveless
-ly	in the manner of	fluently, honestly
-ment	condition, result	document, government
-ness	condition, quality of	willingness, shrewdness, kindness
-or	condition, activity	valor
-ory	a place for	factory, depository, territory
-ous, -ose	full of, characterized by	humorous, courageous, verbose
-ship	status, condition	relationship
-some	characteristic of	loathsome, fearsome, troublesome
-tude	state of being	exactitude
-ure	condition, process, function	exposure
-ward	in a direction or manner	eastward, homeward
-wise	in manner of, with regard	timewise, streetwise
-y	state, condition, result	society, victory

PART III

Notes

Notes

Notes

Notes

Notes

Notes

Notes

Notes

Notes

Notes

Notes